I0832302

THE

POET'S JOURNAL.

BY

BAYARD TAYLOR.

BOSTON:
TICKNOR AND FIELDS.
1863.

SECOND EDITION.

UNIVERSITY PRESS:
WELCH, BIGELOW, AND COMPANY,
CAMBRIDGE.

PREFACE.

THE RETURN OF THE GODDESS.

Not as in youth, with steps outspeeding morn,
  And cheeks all bright, from rapture of the way,
But in strange mood, half cheerful, half forlorn,
          She comes to me to-day.

Does she forget the trysts we used to keep,
  When dead leaves rustled on autumnal ground,
Or the lone garret, whence she banished sleep
          With threats of silver sound?

Does she forget how shone the happy eyes
  When they beheld her, — how the eager tongue
Plied its swift oar through wave-like harmonies,
          To reach her where she sung?

IV

How at her sacred feet I cast me down?
  How she upraised me to her bosom fair,
And from her garland shred the first light crown
    That ever pressed my hair?

Though dust is on the leaves, her breath will bring
  Their freshness back: why lingers she so long?
The pulseless air is waiting for her wing,
    Dumb with unuttered song.

If tender doubt delay her on the road,
  O let her haste to find the doubt belied!
If shame for love unworthily bestowed,
    That shame shall melt in pride.

If she but smile, the crystal calm shall break
  In music, sweeter than it ever gave,
As when a breeze breathes o'er some sleeping lake,
    And laughs in every wave.

The ripples of awakened song shall die
  Kissing her feet, and woo her not in vain,
Until, as once, upon her breast I lie —
    Pardoned, and loved again!

B. T.

CONTENTS.

PAGE
Inscription 7

THE POET'S JOURNAL.

First Evening 9
Darkness 18
The Torso 20
The Dead March 23
On the Headland 25
Marah 27
The Voice of the Tempter 30
Fate Defied 32
Exorcism 34
Squandered Lives 36
Indifference 38
A Symbol 40
Second Evening 47
Atonement 50
December 53
Sylvan Spirits 55
The Lost May 57
Church-Yard Roses 60
Autumnal Dreams 62
In Winter 65
Young Love 67
The Chapel 70
If Love should come again 72

Third Evening 77
The Return of Spring 82
Morning 84
Questions 86
The Vision 88
Love Returned 91
Love Justified 94
A Woman 96
The Count of Gleichen 98
Before the Bridal 101
Possession 103
Under the Moon 105
The Mystic Summer 108
A Watch of the Night 112
The Father 114
The Mother 116
The Family 118

PASSING THE SIRENS 127

VARIOUS POEMS.

Porphyrogenitus 143
The Song of the Camp 146
The Vineyard-Saint 149
Icarus 153
The Bath 158
The Fountain of Trevi 162
My Mission 164
Proposal 167
Renunciation 168
The Quaker Widow 174
Anastasia 181
The Palm and the Pine 182
Over-Possession 186
On Leaving California 188
Euphorion 191
Soldier's Song 195
The Shepherd's Lament 197
The Garden of Roses 199
The Three Songs 203

INSCRIPTION.

TO THE MISTRESS OF CEDARCROFT.

I.

THE evening shadows lengthen on the lawn:
  Westward, our immemorial chestnuts stand,
A mount of shade; but o'er the cedars drawn,
  Between the hedge-row trees, in many a band
Of brightening gold, the sunshine lingers on,
  And soon will touch our oaks with parting hand:
And down the distant valley all is still,
And flushed with purple smiles the beckoning hill.

II.

Come, leave the flowery terrace, leave the beds
  Where Southern children wake to Northern air:
Let yon mimosas droop their tufted heads,
  These myrtle-trees their nuptial beauty wear,

And while the dying day reluctant treads
  From tree-top unto tree-top, with me share
The scene's idyllic peace, the evening's close,
The balm of twilight, and the land's repose.

III.

Come, for my task is done: the task that drew
  My footsteps from the chambers of the Day, —
That held me back, Beloved, even from you,
  That are my daylight: for the Poet's way
Turns into many a lonely avenue
  Where none may follow. He must sing his lay
First to himself, then to the One most dear;
Last, to the world. Come to my side, and hear!

IV.

The poems ripened in a heart at rest,
  A life that first through you is free and strong,
Take them and warm them in your partial breast,
  Before they try the common air of song!
Fame won at home is of all fame the best:
  Crown me your poet, and the critic's wrong
Shall harmless strike where you in love have smiled,
Wife of my heart, and mother of my child!

THE POET'S JOURNAL.

FIRST EVENING.

THE day had come, the day of many years.
My bud of hope, thorned round with guarding fears,
And sealed with frosts of oft-renewed delay,
Burst into sudden bloom — it was the day!
"Ernest will come!" the early sunbeams cried;
"Will come!" was breathed through all the woodlands
wide;
"Will come, will come!" said cloud, and brook, and
bird;
And when the hollow roll of wheels was heard
Across the bridge, it thundered: "He is near!"
And then my heart made answer: "He is here!"

Ernest was here, and now the day had gone
Like other days, yet wild and swift and sweet, —

And yet prolonged, as if with whirling feet
One troop of duplicated Hours sped on,
And one trod out the moments lingeringly:
So distant seemed the lonely dawn from me.
But all was well. He paced the new-mown lawn,
With Edith at his side, and, while my firs
Stood bronzed with sunset, happy glances cast
On the familiar landmarks of the Past.
I heard a gentle laugh: the laugh was hers.
"Confess it," she exclaimed, "I recognize,
No less than you, the features of the place,
So often have I seen it with the eyes
Your memory gave me: yea, your very face,
With every movement of the theme, betrayed
That here the sunshine lay, and there the shade."
"A proof!" cried Ernest. "Let me be your guide,"
She said, "and speak not: Philip shall decide."
To them I went, at beckon of her hand.
A moment she the mellow landscape scanned
In seeming doubt, but only to prolong
A witching aspect of uncertainty,
And the soft smile in Ernest's watching eye:
"Yonder," she said, "(I see I am not wrong,
By Philip's face,) you built your hermit seat
Against the rock, among the scented fern,
Where summer lizards played about your feet;

And here, beside us, is the tottering urn
You cracked in fixing firmly on its base;
And here — yes, yes! — this is the very place —
I know the wild vine and the sassafras —
Where you and Philip, lying in the grass,
Disowned the world, renounced the race of men,
And you all love, except your own for him,
Until, through that, all love came back again."
Here Edith paused; but Ernest's eyes were dim.
He kissed her, gave a loving hand to me,
And spoke: "Ah, Philip, Philip, those were days
We *dare* remember now, when only blaze
Far-off, the storm's black edges brokenly.
Who thinks, at night, that morn will ever be?
Who knows, far out upon the central sea,
That anywhere is land? And yet, a shore
Has set behind us, and will rise before:
A past foretells a future." "Blessed be
That Past!" I answered, "on whose bosom lay
Peace, like a new-born child: and now, I see,
The child is man, begetting day by day
Some fresher joy, some other bliss, to make
Your life the fairer for his mother's sake."

Deeper beneath the oaks the shadows grew:
The twilight glimmer from their tops withdrew,

And purple gloomed the distant hills, and sweet
The sudden breath of evening rose, with balm
Of grassy meadows : in the upper calm
The pulses of the stars began to beat :
The fire-flies twinkled : through the lindens went
A rustle, as of happy leaves composed
To airy sleep, of drowsy petals closed,
And the dark land lay silent and content.
We, too, were silent. Ernest walked, I knew,
With me, beneath the stars of other eves :
He heard, with me, the tongues of perished leaves :
Departed suns their trails of splendor drew
Across departed summers : whispers came
From voices, long ago resolved again
Into the primal Silence, and we twain,
Ghosts of our present selves, yet still the same,
As in a spectral mirror wandered there.
Its pain outlived, the Past was only fair.

Ten years had passed since I had touched his hand,
And felt upon my lips the brother-kiss
That shames not manhood, — years of quiet bliss
To me, fast-rooted on paternal land,
Mated, yet childless. He had journeyed far
Beyond the borders of my life, and whirled
Unresting round the vortex of the world,

The reckless child of some eccentric star,
Careless of fate, yet with a central strength
I knew would hold his life in equipoise,
And bend his wandering energies, at length,
To the smooth orbit of serener joys.
Few were the winds that wafted to my nest
A leaf from him: I learned that he was blest, —
The late fulfilment of my prophecy, —
And then I felt that he must come to me,
The old, unswerving sympathy to claim;
And set my house in order for a guest
Long ere the message of his coming came.

In gentle terraces my garden fell
Down to the rolling lawn. On one side rose,
Flanking the layers of bloom, a bolder swell
With laurels clad, and every shrub that grows
Upon our native hills, a bosky mound,
Whence the commingling valleys might be seen
Bluer and lovelier through the gaps of green.
The rustic arbor which the summit crowned
Was woven of shining smilax, trumpet-vine,
Clematis, and the wild white eglantine,
Whose tropical luxuriance overhung
The interspaces of the posts, and made
For each sweet picture frames of bloom and shade.

It was my favorite haunt when I was young,
To read my poets, watch my sunset fade
Behind my father's hills, and, when the moon
Shed warmer silver through the nights of June,
Dream, as 't were new, the universal dream.
This arbor, too, was Ernest's hermitage:
Here he had read to me his tear-stained page
Of sorrow, here renewed the pang supreme
Which burned his youth to ashes: here would try
To lay his burden in the hands of Song,
And make the Poet bear the Lover's wrong,
But still his heart impatiently would cry:
"In vain, in vain! You cannot teach to flow
In measured lines so measureless a woe.
First learn to slay this wild beast of despair,
Then from his harmless jaws your honey tear!"

Hither we came. Beloved hands had graced
The table with a flask of mellow juice,
Thereto the gentle herb that poets use
When Fancy droops, and in the corner placed
A lamp, that glimmered through its misty sphere
Like moonlit marble, on a pedestal
Of knotted roots, against the leafy wall.
The air was dry, the night was calm and clear,
And in the dying clover crickets chirped.

The Past, I felt, the Past alone usurped
Our thoughts, — the hour of confidence had come,
Of sweet confession, tender interchange,
Which drew our hearts together, yet with strange
Half-dread repelled them. Seeing Ernest dumb
With memories of the spot, as if to me
Belonged the right his secrets to evoke,
And Edith's eyes on mine, consentingly,
Conscious of all I wished to know, I spoke:
" Dear Friend, one volume of your life I read
Beneath these vines: you placed it in my hand
And made it mine, — but how the tale has sped
Since then, I know not, or can understand
From this fair ending only. Let me see
The intervening chapters, dark and bright,
In order, as you lived them. Give to-night
Unto the Past, dear Ernest, and to me!"
Thus I, with doubt and loving hesitance,
Lest I should touch a nerve he fain would hide;
But he, with calm and reassuring glance,
In which no troubled shadow lay, replied:
" That mingled light and darkness are no more
In this new life, than are the sun and shade
Of painted landscapes: distant lies the shore
Where last we parted, Philip: how I made
The journey, what adventures on the road,

What haps I met, what struggles, what success
Of fame, or gold, or place, concerns you less,
Dear friend, than how I lost that sorest load
I started with, and came to dwell at last
In the House Beautiful. There but remains
A fragment here and there, — wild, broken strains
And scattered voices speaking from the Past."
" Let me those broken voices hear," I said,
" And I shall know the rest." " Well — be it so.
You, who would write '*Resurgam*' o'er my dead,
The resurrection of my heart shall know."

Then Edith rose, and up the terraces
Went swiftly to the house; but soon we spied
Her white dress gleam, returning through the trees,
And, softly flushed, she came to Ernest's side,
A volume in her hand. But he delayed
Awhile his task, revolving leaf by leaf
With tender interest, now that ancient grief
No more had power to make his heart afraid;
For pain, that only lives in memory,
Like battle-scars, it is no pain to show.
" Here, Philip, are the secrets you would know,"
He said: " Howe'er obscure the utterance be,
The lamp you lighted in the olden time
Will show my heart's-blood beating through the rhyme:

A poet's journal, writ in fire and tears
At first, blind protestations, blinder rage,
(For you and Edith only, many a page !)
Then slow deliverance, with the gaps of years
Between, and final struggles into life,
Which the heart shrank from, as 't were death instead."
Then, with a loving glance towards his wife,
Which she as fondly answered, thus he read :—

DARKNESS.

THE thread I held has slipped from out my hand:
  In this dark labyrinth, without a clew,
Groping for guidance, stricken blind, I stand,
  A helpless child that knows not what to do.

When all the glory of the morn was mine,
  The sudden night surprised me unawares:
I see no pitying star above me shine,
  I hear no voice in answer to my prayers.

At every step, I stumble on the road;
  Fain would I rest, the wild hours whirl me on;
What business have I in this blank abode,
  Whence Love, and Hope, and even Faith, are gone?

A child of summer, shivering in the cold,—
  A son of light, by darkness overcome,—
A bird of air, my broken wings I fold,
  A harp of joy, my shattered strings are dumb.

And every gift that Life to me had given
  Lies at my feet, in useless fragments trod:
There is no justice or in Earth or Heaven:
  There is no pity in the heart of God.

THE TORSO.

I.

IN clay the statue stood complete,
  As beautiful a form, and fair,
As ever walked a Roman street
  Or breathed the blue Athenian air:
  The perfect limbs, divinely bare,
Their old, heroic freedom kept,
  And in the features, fine and rare,
A calm, immortal sweetness slept.

II.

O'er common men it towered, a god,
  And smote their meaner life with shame,
For while its feet the highway trod,
  Its lifted brow was crowned with flame

And purified from touch of blame:
Yet wholly human was the face,
And over them who saw it came
The knowledge of their own disgrace.

III.

It stood, regardless of the crowd,
And simply showed what men might be:
Its solemn beauty disavowed
The curse of lost humanity.
Erect and proud, and pure and free,
It overlooked each loathsome law
Whereunto others bend the knee,
And only what was noble saw.

IV.

The patience and the hope of years
Their final hour of triumph caught;
The clay was tempered with my tears,
The forces of my spirit wrought
With hands of fire to shape my thought,
That when, complete, the statue stood,
To marble resurrection brought,
The Master might pronounce it good.

V.

But in the night an enemy,
  Who could not bear the wreath should grace
My ready forehead, stole the key
  And hurled my statue from its base;
  And now its fragments strew the place
Where I had dreamed its shrine might be:
  The stains of common earth deface
Its beauty and its majesty.

VI.

The torso prone before me lies;
  The cloven brow is knit with pain:
Mute lips, and blank, reproachful eyes
  Unto my hands appeal in vain.
  My hands shall never work again:
My hope is dead, my strength is spent:
  This fatal wreck shall now remain
The ruined sculptor's monument.

THE DEAD MARCH.

I.

The April sky with sunshine filled the street,
And lightly fell the tread of pattering feet,
  As on the last year's leaves the April rain.
The glaring houses wore a foreign grace;
A foreign sweetness shone on Labor's face,
  And open lay, relaxed, the hand of Gain.

II.

My sorrow slept; I breathed the peace of Spring.
One fledgeling hope outreached a timorous wing:
  Concealed, at least, and sacred was my pain, —
When, suddenly, the dreadful trumpets blew,
And every wind my gloomy secret knew,
  And all the echoes hurled it back again.

III.

Before a stranger's corpse the trumpets cried
So bitterly, it seemed all love had died:
  Then hollow horns took up the fatal strain,
Till tongues of fire went flashing through the air,
The myriad clamors of a sole despair,
  The cry of grief that knows its cry is vain.

IV.

The dead was fortunate, — he could not hear:
The mourners comforted, behind his bier:
  Through happy crowds advanced the funeral train:
Mine was the sorrow, mine the deathlike pang,
And tears, that burned the eyelids as they sprang,
  To hear the awful music of my pain.

ON THE HEADLAND.

I SIT on the lonely headland,
Where the sea-gulls come and go:
The sky is gray above me,
And the sea is gray below.

There is no fisherman's pinnace
Homeward or outward bound;
I see no living creature
In the world's deserted round.

I pine for something human,
Man, woman, young or old, —
Something to meet and welcome,
Something to clasp and hold.

I have a mouth for kisses,
But there 's no one to give and take;
I have a heart in my bosom
Beating for nobody's sake.

O warmth of love that is wasted!
  Is there none to stretch a hand?
No other heart that hungers
  In all the living land?

I could fondle the fisherman's baby,
  And rock it into rest;
I could take the sunburnt sailor,
  Like a brother, to my breast.

I could clasp the hand of any
  Outcast of land or sea,
If the guilty palm but answered
  The tenderness in me!

The sea might rise and drown me, —
  Cliffs fall and crush my head, —
Were there one to love me, living,
  Or weep to see me dead!

MARAH.

THE waters of my life were sweet,
  Before that bolt of sorrow fell;
But now, though fainting with the heat,
  I dare not drink the bitter well.

My God! shall Sin across the heart
  Sweep like a wind that leaves no trace,
But Grief inflict a rankling smart
  No after blessing can efface?

I see the tired mechanic take
  His evening rest beside his door,
And gentlier, for their father's sake,
  His children tread the happy floor:

The kitchen teems with cheering smells,
  With clash of cups and clink of knives,
And all the household picture tells
  Of humble yet contented lives.

Then in my heart the serpents hiss:
  What right have these, who scarcely know
The perfect sweetness of their bliss,
  To flaunt it thus before my woe?

Like bread, Love's portion they divide,
  Like water drink his precious wine,
When the least crumb they cast aside
  Were manna for these lips of mine.

I see the friend of other days
  Lead home his flushed and silent bride:
His eyes are suns of tender praise,
  Her eyes are stars of tender pride.

Go, hide your shameless happiness,
  The demon cries, within my breast;
Think not that I the bond can bless,
  Which seeing, I am twice unblest.

The husband of a year proclaims
  His recent honor, shows the boy,
And calls the babe a thousand names,
  And dandles it in awkward joy:

And then — I see the wife's pale cheek,
  Her eyes of pure, celestial ray —
The curse is choked: I cannot speak,
  But, weeping, turn my head away!

THE VOICE OF THE TEMPTER.

LAST night the Tempter came to me, and said:
"Why sorrow any longer for the dead?
The wrong is done: thy tears and groans are naught:
Forget the Past, — thy pain but lives in thought.
Night after night, I hear thy cries implore
An answer: she will answer thee no more.
Give up thine idle prayer that Death may come
And thou mayst somewhere find her: Death is dumb
To those that seek him. Live: for youth is thine.
Let not thy rich blood, like neglected wine,
Grow thin and stale, but rouse thyself, at last,
And take a man's revenge upon the Past.
What have thy virtues brought thee? Let them go,
And with them lose the burden of thy woe,
Their only payment for thy service hard:
They but exact, thou see'st, and not reward.

Thy life is cheated, thou art cast aside
In dust, the worn-out vessel of their pride.
Come, take thy pleasure: others do the same,
And love is theirs, and fortune, name and fame!
Let not the name of Vice thine ear affright:
Vice is no darkness, but a different light,
Which thou dost need, to see thy path aright;
Or if some pang in this experience lie,
Through counter-pain thy present pain will die.
Bethink thee of the lost, the barren years,
Of harsh privations, unavailing tears,
The steady ache of strong desires restrained,
And what thou hast deserved, and what obtained:
Then go, thou fool! and, if thou canst, rejoice
To make such base ingratitude thy choice,
While each indulgence which thy brethren taste,
But mocks thy palate, as it runs to waste!"

So spake the Tempter, as he held outspread
Alluring pictures round my prostrate head.
'Twixt sleep and waking, in my helpless ear
His honeyed voice rang musical and clear;
And half persuaded, shaken half with fear,
I heard him, till the Morn began to shine,
And found her brow less dewy-wet than mine.

FATE DEFIED.

If seed was meant to grow, or buds to swell
  In vernal airs, or birds to mate and build,
  Then this quick love, wherewith my heart is filled,
Was meant to bourgeon and to bloom, as well.

If sap was made, to mount in every tree,
  And blood, to fill the million veins of man,
  Then I was made, the hour my life began,
To share the universal destiny.

If, as ordained, each creature finds his mate
  And gives to younger lamps his fading flame
  Of life, then I a like fulfilment claim,
Nor ask release from my appointed fate.

This heart is flesh, I cannot make it stone:
  This blood is hot, I cannot stop its flow:
  These arms are vacant — wheresoe'er I go,
Love lies in others' arms, and shuns my own.

I who have waited, served, performed my task
  For seven long years, and find my Rachel fled,
  What recompense shall now be mine instead?
Fate turns away, nor grants the least I ask!

Come, 't is enough! — Fate, Law, whatever rules
  This wretched Earth, my hand is on thy throat:
  Pour on these wounds the sole sweet antidote,
And keep thy tricks for cowards and for fools!

Too long I 've lain, and with submissive will
  Suffered: my rights I now demand of thee:
  Give me the wife, the home, thou stol'st from me,
The children of the Future thou didst kill!

Mine thou hast chosen from a thousand lives
  To bear thy malice: cruel Power, take heed!
  Pierced unto death, the conquered heart may bleed, —
The vengeance of an injured man survives.

Give back, thou thief, thy plunder! Let me lie
  In some low nook of earth, obscure, forgot,
  But sharing still my brethren's blessed lot,
Or I will wrestle with thee till I die!

EXORCISM.

O, TONGUES of the Past, be still!
Are the days not over and gone?
The joys have perished that were so sweet,
But the sorrow still lives on.

I have sealed the graves of my hopes;
I have carried the pall of love:
Let the pains and pangs be buried as deep,
And the grass be as green above!

But the ghosts of the dead arise:
They come when the board is spread:
They poison the wine of the banquet cups
With the mould their lips have shed.

The pulse of the bacchant blood
May throb in the ivy wreath,
But the berries are plucked from the nightshade bough
That grows in the gardens of Death.

I sleep with joy at my heart,
   Warm as a new-made bride;
But a vampyre comes to suck her blood,
   And I wake with a corpse at my side.

Shall I open your fatal graves?
   Shall I drive a stake through the clay,
Till ye cease to drain from my bankrupt veins
   The life ye have made your prey?

O ghosts, I have given to you
   The bliss of the faded years;
The sweat of my brow, the blood of my heart,
   And manhood's terrible tears!

Take them, and be content:
   I have nothing more to give:
My soul is chilled in the house of Death,
   And 't is time that I should live.

Take them, and let me be:
   Lie still in the churchyard mould,
Nor chase from my heart each new delight
   With the phantom of the old!

SQUANDERED LIVES.

The fisherman wades in the surges;
  The sailor sails over the sea;
The soldier steps bravely to battle;
  The woodman lays axe to the tree.

They are each of the breed of the heroes,
  The manhood attempered in strife:
Strong hands, that go lightly to labor,
  True hearts, that take comfort in life.

In each is the seed to replenish
  The world with the vigor it needs, —
The centre of honest affections,
  The impulse to generous deeds.

But the shark drinks the blood of the fisher;
  The sailor is dropped in the sea;
The soldier lies cold by his cannon;
  The woodman is crushed by his tree.

Each prodigal life that is wasted
  In manly achievement unseen,
But lengthens the days of the coward,
  And strengthens the crafty and mean.

The blood of the noblest is lavished
  That the selfish a profit may find ;
But God sees the lives that are squandered,
  And we to His wisdom are blind.

INDIFFERENCE.

I.

We Fools! that meekly take the bit
  And drag the burden all our lives!
Poor, blinded steeds, we all submit,
Nor know our load, scarce seeing it,
Although with stinging lash Fate goads us as she drives.

II.

What does it help, the gold we bear,
  When we are worn, and halt, and lean?
No fresher tastes the dusty air
When Fame's triumphant trumpets blare,
And we the road would leave, to lie in pastures green.

III.

Nor profits much a virtuous name,
So short a time the crown we wear:
In fifty years 't will be the same
As if it were a crown of shame,
For none will know our lives, or, if they knew, would care.

IV.

Life came to me: why should I take
The tasks I did not seek to do?
I did them for another's sake
In vain: and now the yoke I break,
And let the world roll on, regardless of its crew.

V.

Here, take my days, whatever Fate
The worthless gift may choose to claim;
For I am weary of their weight:
Alike to me is love or hate:
Do with me as you please, all fortunes are the same.

A SYMBOL.

I.

HEAVY, and hot, and gray,
Day following unto day,
A felon gang, their blind life drag away, —

Blind, vacant, dumb, as Time,
Lapsed from his wonted prime,
Begot them basely in incestuous crime:

So little life there seems
About the woods and streams, —
Only a sleep, perplexed with nightmare-dreams.

The burden of a sigh
Stifles the weary sky,
Where smouldering clouds in ashen masses lie:

The forests fain would groan,
But, silenced into stone,
Crouch, in the dull blue vapors round them thrown.

O light, more drear than gloom!
Than death more dead such bloom:
Yet life — yet life — shall burst this gathering doom!

II.

Behold! a swift and silent fire
Yon dull cloud pierces, in the west,
And blackening, as with growing ire,
He lifts his forehead from his breast.

He mutters to the ashy host
That all around him sleeping lie, —
Sole chieftain on the airy coast,
To fight the battles of the sky.

He slowly lifts his weary strength,
His shadow rises on the day,
And distant forests feel at length
A wind from landscapes far away.

III.

How shall the cloud unload its thunder?
  How shall its flashes fire the air?
Hills and valleys are dumb with wonder:
  Lakes look up with a leaden stare.

Hark! the lungs of the striding giant
  Bellow an angry answer back!
Hurling the hair from his brows defiant,
  Crushing the laggards along his track,

Now his step, like a battling Titan's,
  Scales in flame the hills of the sky;
Struck by his breath, the forest whitens;
  Fluttering waters feel him nigh!

Stroke on stroke of his thunder-hammer —
  Sheets of flame from his anvil hurled —
Heaven's doors are burst in the clamor:
  He alone possesses the world!

IV.

Drowned woods, shudder no more:
Vexed lakes, smile as before:

Hills that vanished, appear again:
Rise for harvest, prostrate grain!

Shake thy jewels, twinkling grass:
Blossoms, tint the winds that pass:
Sun, behold a world restored!
World, again thy sun is lord!

Thunder-spasms the waking be
Into Life from Apathy:
Life, not Death, is in the gale,—
Let the coming Doom prevail!

THUS far he read: at first with even tone,
Still chanting in the old, familiar key,—
That golden note, whose grand monotony
Is musical in poets' mouths alone,—
But broken, as he read, became the chime.
To speak, once more, in Grief's forgotten tongue,
And feel the hot reflex of passion flung
Back on the heart by every pulse of rhyme
Wherein it lives and burns, a soul might shake
More calm than his. With many a tender break
Of voice, a dimness of the haughty eye,
And pause of wandering memory, he read;
While I, with folded arms and downcast head,
In silence heard each blind, bewildered cry.

Thus far had Ernest read: but, closing now
The book, and lifting up a calmer brow,
"Forgive me, patient God, for this!" he said:
"And you forgive, dear friend, and dearest wife,
If I have marred an hour of this sweet life
With noises from the valley of the Dead.

Long, long ago, the Hand whereat I railed
In blindness gave me courage to subdue
This wild revolt: I see wherein I failed:
My heart was false, when most I thought it true,
My sorrow selfish, when I thought it pure.
For those we lose, if still their love endure
Translation to that other land where Love
Breathes the immortal wisdom, ask in heaven
No greater sacrifice than we had given
On earth, our love's integrity to prove.
If we are blest to know the other blest,
Then treason lies in sorrow. Vainly said!
Alone each heart must cover up its dead;
Alone, through bitter toil, achieve its rest:
Which I have found — but still these records keep,
Lest I, condemning others, should forget
My own rebellion. From these tares I reap,
In evil days, a fruitful harvest yet.

"But 't is enough, to-night. Nay, Philip, here
A chapter closes. See! the moon is near:
Your laurels glitter: come, my darling, sing
The hymn I wrote on such a night as this!"
Then Edith, stooping first to take his kiss,
Drew from its niche of woodbine her guitar,
With chords prelusive tuned a slackened string,

And sang, clear-voiced, as some melodious star
Were dropping silver sweetness from afar:

God, to whom we look up blindly,
Look Thou down upon us kindly:
We have sinned, but not designedly.

If our faith in Thee was shaken,
Pardon Thou our hearts mistaken,
Our obedience reawaken.

We are sinful, Thou art holy:
Thou art mighty, we are lowly:
Let us reach Thee, climbing slowly.

Our ingratitude confessing,
On Thy mercy still transgressing,
Thou dost punish us with blessing!

SECOND EVENING.

It was the evening of the second day,
Which swifter, sweeter than the first had fled:
My heart's delicious tumult passed away,
And left a sober happiness instead.
For Ernest's voice was ever in mine ear,
His presence mingled as of old with mine,
But stronger, manlier, brighter, more divine
Its effluence now: within his starry sphere
Of love new-risen my nature too was drawn,
And warmed with rosy flushes of the dawn.

All day we drove about the lovely vales,
Under the hill-side farms, through summer woods, —
The land of mingled homes and solitudes
That Ernest loved. We told the dear old tales
Of childhood, music new to Edith's ear,
Sang olden songs, lived old adventures o'er,
And, when the hours brought need of other cheer,

Spread on the ferny rocks a tempting store
Of country dainties. 'T was our favorite dell,
Cut by the trout-stream through a wooded ridge:
Above, the highway on a mossy bridge
Strode o'er it, and below, the water fell
Through hornblende bowlders, where the dircus flung
His pliant rods, the berried spice-wood grew,
And tulip-trees and smooth magnolias hung
A million leaves between us and the blue.
The silver water-dust in puffs arose
And turned to dust of jewels in the sun,
And like a canon, in its close begun
Afresh, the stream's perpetual lullaby
Sang down the dell, and deepened its repose.
Here, till the western hours had left the sky,
We sat: then homeward loitered through the dusk
Of chestnut woods, along the meadow-side,
And lost in lanes that breathed ambrosial musk
Of wild-grape blossoms: and the twilight died.

Long after every star came out, we paced
The terrace, still discoursing on the themes
The day had started, intermixed with dreams
Born of the summer night. Then, golden-faced,
Behind her daybreak of auroral gleams,
The moon arose: the bosom of the lawn

Whitened beneath her silent snow of light,
Save where the trees made isles of mystic night,
Dark blots against the rising splendor drawn,
And where the eastern wall of woodland towered,
Blue darkness, filled with undistinguished shapes:
But elsewhere, over all the landscape showered —
A silver drizzle on the distant capes
Of hills — the glory of the moon. We sought,
Drawn thither by the same unspoken thought,
The mound, where now the leaves of laurel clashed
Their dagger-points of light, around the bower,
And through the nets of leaf and elfin flower,
Cold fire, the sprinkled drops of moonshine flashed.

Erelong in Ernest's hand the volume lay,
(I did not need a second time to ask,)
And he resumed the intermitted task.
" This night, dear Philip, is the Poet's day,"
He said : " the world is one confessional:
Our sacred memories as freely fall
As leaves from o'er-ripe blossoms: we betray
Ourselves to Nature, who the tale can win
We shrink from uttering in the daylight's din.
So, Friend, come back with me a little way
Along the years, and in these records find
The sole inscriptions they have left behind."

ATONEMENT.

If thou hadst died at midnight,
  With a lamp beside thy bed;
The beauty of sleep exchanging
  For the beauty of the dead:

When the bird of heaven had called thee,
  And the time had come to go,
And the northern lights were dancing
  On the dim December snow —

If thou hadst died at midnight,
  I had ceased to bid thee stay,
Hearing the feet of the Father
  Leading His child away.

I had knelt, in the awful Presence,
  And covered my guilty head,
And received His absolution
  For my sins toward the dead.

But the cruel sun was shining
  In the cold and windy sky,
And Life, with his mocking voices,
  Looked in to see thee die.

God came and went unheeded;
  No tear repentant shone;
And he took the heart from my bosom,
  And left in its place a stone.

Each trivial promise broken,
  Each tender word unsaid,
Must be evermore unspoken, —
  Unpardoned by the dead.

Unpardoned? No: the struggle
  Of years was not in vain, —
The patience that wearies passion,
  And the prayers that conquer pain.

This tardy resignation
  May be the blessed sign
Of pardon and atonement,
  Thy spirit sends to mine.

Now first I dare remember
  That day of death and woe:
Within, the dreadful silence,
  Without, the sun and snow!

DECEMBER.

THE beech is bare, and bare the ash,
  The thickets white below;
The fir-tree scowls with hoar moustache,
  He cannot sing for snow.

The body-guard of veteran pines,
  A grim battalion, stands;
They ground their arms, in ordered lines,
  For Winter so commands.

The waves are dumb along the shore,
  The river's pulse is still;
The north-wind's bugle blows no more
  Reveillé from the hill.

The rustling sift of falling snow,
  The muffled crush of leaves,
These are the sounds suppressed, that show
  How much the forest grieves;

But, as the blind and vacant Day
   Crawls to his ashy bed,
I hear dull echoes far away,
   Like drums above the dead.

Sigh with me, Pine that never changed!
   Thou wear'st the Summer's hue;
Her other loves are all estranged,
   But thou and I are true!

SYLVAN SPIRITS.

The gray stems rise, the branches braid
A covering of deepest shade.
Beneath these old, inviolate trees
There comes no stealthy, sliding breeze,
To overhear their mysteries.

Steeped in the fragrant breath of leaves,
My heart a hermit peace receives:
The sombre forest thrusts a screen
My refuge and the world between,
And beds me in its balmy green.

No fret of life may here intrude,
To vex the sylvan solitude.
Pure spirits of the earth and air,
From hollow trunk and bosky lair
Come forth, and hear your lover's prayer!

Come, Druid soul of ancient oak,
Thou, too, hast felt the thunder-stroke;

Come, Hamadryad of the beech,
Nymph of the burning maple, teach
My heart the solace of your speech!

Alas! the sylvan ghosts preserve
The natures of the race they serve.
Not only Dryads, chaste and shy,
But piping Fauns, come dancing nigh,
And Satyrs of the shaggy thigh.

Across the calm, the holy hush
And shadowed air, there darts a flush
Of riot, from the lawless brood,
And rebel voices in my blood
Salute these orgies of the wood.

Not sacred thoughts alone engage
The saint in silent hermitage:
The soul within him heavenward strives,
Yet strong, as in profaner lives,
The giant of the flesh survives.

From Nature, as from human haunts,
That giant draws his sustenance.
By her own elves, in woodlands wild
She sees her robes of prayer defiled:
She is not purer than her child.

THE LOST MAY.

WHEN May, with cowslip-braided locks,
  Walks through the land in green attire,
And burns in meadow-grass the phlox
    His torch of purple fire:

When buds have burst the silver sheath,
  And shifting pink, and gray, and gold
Steal o'er the woods, while fair beneath
    The bloomy vales unfold:

When, emerald-bright, the hemlock stands
  New-feathered, needled new the pine;
And, exiles from the orient lands,
    The turbaned tulips shine:

When wild azaleas deck the knoll,
  And cinque-foil stars the fields of home,
And winds, that take the white-weed, roll
    The meadows into foam:

Then from the jubilee I turn
  To other Mays that I have seen,
Where more resplendent blossoms burn,
    And statelier woods are green; —

Mays, when my heart expanded first,
  A honeyed blossom, fresh with dew;
And one sweet wind of heaven dispersed
    The only clouds I knew.

For she, whose softly-murmured name
  The music of the month expressed,
Walked by my side, in holy shame
    Of girlish love confessed.

The budding chestnuts overhead,
  Their sprinkled shadows in the lane, —
Blue flowers along the brooklet's bed, —
    I see them all again!

The old, old tale of girl and boy,
  Repeated ever, never old :
To each in turn the gates of joy,
    The gates of heaven unfold.

And when the punctual May arrives,
  With cowslip-garland on her brow,
We know what once she gave our lives,
    And cannot give us now !

CHURCH-YARD ROSES.

THE woodlands wore a gloomy green,
The tawny stubble clad the hill,
And August hung her smoky screen
Above the valleys, hot and still.

No life was in the fields that day;
My steps were safe from curious eyes:
I wandered where, in church-yard clay,
The dust of love and beauty lies.

Around me thrust the nameless graves
Their fatal ridges, side by side,
So green, they seemed but grassy waves,
Yet quiet as the dead they hide.

And o'er each pillow of repose
Some innocent memento grew,
Of pansy, pink, or lowly rose,
Or hyssop, lavender, and rue.

What flower is hers, the maiden bride?
  What sacred plant protects her bed?
I saw, the greenest mound beside,
  A rose of dark and lurid red.

An eye of fierce demoniac stain,
  It mocked my calm and chastened grief;
I tore it, stung with sudden pain,
  And stamped in earth each bloody leaf

And down upon that trampled grave
  In recklessness my body cast:
"Give back the life I could not save,
  Or give deliverance from the Past!"

But something gently touched my cheek,
  Caressing while its touch reproved:
A rose, all white and snowy-meek,
  It grew upon the dust I loved!

A breeze the holy blossom pressed
  Upon my lips: dear Saint, I cried,
Still blooms the white rose, in my breast,
  Of Love that Death has sanctified!

AUTUMNAL DREAMS.

I.

WHEN the maple turns to crimson
  And the sassafras to gold;
When the gentian 's in the meadow,
  And the aster on the wold;
When the noon is lapped in vapor
  And the night is frosty-cold:

II.

When the chestnut-burs are opened,
  And the acorns drop like hail,
And the drowsy air is startled
  With the thumping of the flail,—
With the drumming of the partridge
  And the whistle of the quail:

III.

Through the rustling woods I wander,
  Through the jewels of the year,
From the yellow uplands calling,
  Seeking her that still is dear:
She is near me in the autumn,
  She, the beautiful, is near.

IV.

Through the smoke of burning summer,
  When the weary winds are still,
I can see her in the valley,
  I can hear her on the hill,—
In the splendor of the woodlands,
  In the whisper of the rill.

V.

For the shores of Earth and Heaven
  Meet, and mingle in the blue:
She can wander down the glory
  To the places that she knew,
Where the happy lovers wandered
  In the days when life was true.

VI.

So I think, when days are sweetest,
  And the world is wholly fair,
She may sometime steal upon me
  Through the dimness of the air,
With the cross upon her bosom
  And the amaranth in her hair.

VII.

Once to meet her, ah! to meet her,
  And to hold her gently fast
Till I blessed her, till she blessed me, —
  That were happiness, at last:
That were bliss beyond our meetings
  In the autumns of the Past!

IN WINTER.

The valley stream is frozen,
  The hills are cold and bare,
And the wild white bees of winter
  Swarm in the darkened air.

I look on the naked forest:
  Was it ever green in June?
Did it burn with gold and crimson
  In the dim autumnal noon?

I look on the barren meadow:
  Was it ever heaped with hay?
Did it hide the grassy cottage
  Where the skylark's children lay?

I look on the desolate garden:
  Is it true the rose was there?
And the woodbine's musky blossoms,
  And the hyacinth's purple hair?

E

I look on my heart, and marvel
  If Love were ever its own, —
If the spring of promise brightened,
  And the summer of passion shone?

Is the stem of bliss but withered,
  And the root survives the blast?
Are the seeds of the Future sleeping
  Under the leaves of the Past?

Ah, yes! for a thousand Aprils
  The frozen germs shall grow,
And the dews of a thousand summers
  Wait in the womb of the snow!

YOUNG LOVE.

We are not old, we are not cold,
  Our hearts are warm and tender yet;
Our arms are eager to enfold
  More bounteous love than we have met.

Still many another heart lays bare
  Its secret chamber to our eyes,
Though dim with passion's lurid air,
  Or pure as morns of Paradise.

They give the love, whose glory lifts
  Desire beyond the realm of sense;
They make us rich with lavish gifts,
  The wealth of noble confidence.

We must be happy, must be proud,
  So crowned with human trust and truth;
But ah! the love that first we vowed,
  The dear religion of our youth!

Voluptuous bloom and fragrance rare
  The summer to its rose may bring;
Far sweeter to the wooing air
  The hidden violet of the spring.

Still, still that lovely ghost appears,
  Too fair, too pure, to bid depart;
No riper love of later years
  Can steal its beauty from the heart.

O splendid sun that shone above!
  O green magnificence of Earth!
Born once into that land of love,
  No life can know a second birth.

Dear, boyish heart, that trembled so
  With bashful fear and fond unrest,—
More frightened than a dove, to know
  Another bird within its nest!

Sharp thrills of doubt, wild hopes that came,
  Fond words addressed,—each word a pang:
Then—hearts, baptized in heavenly flame,
  How like the morning stars ye sang!

Love bound ye with his holiest link,
  The faith in each that asks no more,
And led ye from the sacred brink
  Of mysteries he held in store.

Love led ye, children, from the bowers
  Where Strength and Beauty find his crown:
Ye were not ripe for mortal flowers;
  God's angel brought an amaranth down.

Our eyes are dim with fruitless tears,
  Our eyes are dim, our hearts are sore:
That lost religion of our years
  Comes never, never, nevermore!

THE CHAPEL.

LIKE one who leaves the trampled street
For some cathedral, cool and dim,
Where he can hear in music beat
The heart of prayer, that beats for him ;

And sees the common light of day,
Through painted panes transfigured, shine,
And casts his human woes away,
In presence of the Woe Divine :

So I, from life's tormenting themes
Turn where the silent chapel lies,
Whose windows burn with vanished dreams,
Whose altar-lights are memories.

There, watched by pitying cherubim,
In sacred hush, I rest awhile,
Till solemn sounds of harp and hymn
Begin to sweep the haunted aisle :

A hymn that once but breathed complaint,
  And breathes but resignation now,
Since God has heard the pleading saint,
  And laid His hand upon my brow.

Restored and comforted, I go
  To grapple with my tasks again;
Through silent worship taught to know
  The blessed peace that follows pain.

IF LOVE SHOULD COME AGAIN.

If Love should come again, I ask my heart
In tender tremors, not unmixed with pain,
Couldst thou be calm, nor feel thine ancient smart,
If Love should come again?

Couldst thou unbar the chambers where his nest
So long was made, and made, alas! in vain,
Nor with embarrassed welcome chill thy guest,
If Love should come again?

Would Love his ruined quarters recognize,
Where shrouded pictures of the Past remain,
And gently turn them with forgiving eyes,
If Love should come again?

Would bliss, in milder type, spring up anew,
As silent craters with the scarlet stain
Of flowers repeat the lava's ancient hue,
If Love should come again?

Would Fate, relenting, sheathe the cruel blade
  Whereby the angel of thy youth was slain,
That thou might'st all possess him, unafraid,
    If Love should come again?

In vain I ask: my heart makes no reply,
  But echoes evermore the sweet refrain;
Till, trembling lest it seem a wish, I sigh:
    If Love should come again!

" THE darkness and the twilight have an end,"
Said Ernest, as he laid the book aside,
And, with a tenderness he could not hide,
Smiled, seeing in the eyes of wife and friend
The same soft dew that made his own so dim.
My heart was strangely moved, but not for him.
The holy night, the stars that twinkled faint,
Serfs of the regnant moon, the slumbering trees
And silvery hills, recalled fair memories
Of her I knew, his life's translated saint,
Who seemed too sacred now, too far removed,
To be by him lamented or beloved.
And yet she stood, I knew, by Ernest's side
Invisible, a glory in the heart,
A light of peace, the inner counterpart
Of that which round us poured its radiant tide.

We sat in silence, till a wind, astray
From some uneasy planet, shook the vines
And sprinkled us with snow of eglantines.
The laurels rustled as it passed away,
And, million-tongued, the woodland whisper crept

Of leaves that turned in sleep, from tree to tree
All down the lawn, and once again they slept.
Then Edith from her tender fantasy
Awoke, yet still her pensive posture kept,
Her white hands motionless upon her knee,
Her eyes upon a star that sparkled through
The mesh of leaves, and hummed a wandering air,
(As if the music of her thought it were,)
Low, sweet, and sad, until to words it grew
That made it sweeter, — words that Ernest knew :

Love, I follow, follow thee,
Wipe thine eyes and thou shalt see :
Sorrow makes thee blind to me.

I am with thee, blessing, blest ;
Let thy doubts be laid to rest :
Rise, and take me to thy breast !

In thy bliss my steps behold :
Stretch thine arms and bliss enfold :
'T is thy sorrow makes me cold.

Life is good, and life is fair,
Love awaits thee everywhere :
Love ! is Love's immortal prayer.

Live for love, and thou shalt be,
Loving others, true to me:
Love, I follow, follow thee!

Thus Edith sang: the stars heard, and the night,
The happy spirits, leaning from the wall
Of Heaven, the saints, and God above them all,
Heard what she sang. She ceased: her brow was bright
With other splendor than the moon's: she rose,
Gave each a hand, and silently we trod
The dry, white gravel and the dewy sod,
And silently we parted for repose.

THIRD EVENING.

For days before, the wild-dove cooed for rain.
The sky had been too bright, the world too fair.
We knew such loveliness could not remain :
We heard its ruin by the flattering air
Foretold, that o'er the fields so sweetly blew,
Yet came, at night, a banshee, moaning through
The chimney's throat, and at the window wailed:
We heard the tree-toad trill his piercing note:
The sound seemed near us, when, on farms remote,
The supper-horn the scattered workmen hailed:
Above the roof the eastward-pointing vane
Stood fixed: and still the wild-dove cooed for rain.

So, when the morning came, and found no fire
Upon her hearth, and wrapped her shivering form
In cloud, and rising winds in many a gyre
Of dust foreran the footsteps of the storm,

And woods grew dark, and flowery meadows chill,
And gray annihilation smote the hill,
I said to Ernest: "'T was my plan, you see:
Two days to Nature, and the third to me.
For you must stay, perforce: the day is doomed.
No visitors shall yonder valley find,
Except the spirits of the rain and wind:
Here you must bide, my friends, with me entombed
In this dim crypt, where shelved around us lie
The mummied authors." "Place me, when I die,"
Laughed Ernest, "in as fair a catacomb,
I shall not call posterity unjust,
That leaves my bones in Shakespeare's, Goethe's home,
Like king and beggar mixed in Memphian dust.
But you are right: this day we well may give
To you, dear Philip, and to those who stand
Protecting Nature with a jealous hand,
At once her subjects and her haughty lords;
Since, in the breath of their immortal words
Alone, she first begins to speak and live."

I know not, if that day of dreary rain
Was not the happiest of the happy three.
For Nature gives, but takes away again:
Sound, odor, color — blossom, cloud, and tree
Divide and scatter in a thousand rays

Our individual being: but, in days
Of gloom, the wandering senses crowding come
To the close circle of the heart. So we,
Cosily nestled in the library,
Enjoyed each other and the warmth of home.
Each window was a picture of the rain:
Blown by the wind, tormented, wet, and gray,
Losing itself in cloud, the landscape lay;
Or wavered, blurred, behind the streaming pane;
Or, with a sudden struggle, shook away
Its load, and like a foundering ship arose
Distinct and dark above the driving spray,
Until a fiercer onset came, to close
The hopeless day. The roses writhed about
Their stakes, the tall laburnums to and fro
Rocked in the gusts, the flowers were beaten low,
And from his pigmy house the wren looked out
With dripping bill: each living creature fled,
To seek some sheltering cover for its head:
Yet colder, drearier, wilder as it blew,
We drew the closer, and the happier grew.

She with her needle, he with pipe and book,
My guests contented sat: my cheerful dame,
Intent on household duties, went and came,
And I unto my childless bosom took

The little two-year Arthur, Ernest's child,
A darling boy, to both his parents true, —
With father's brow, and mother's eyes of blue,
And the same dimpled beauty when he smiled.
Ah me! the father's heart within me woke:
The child that never was, I seemed to hold:
The withered tenderness that bloomed of old
In vain, revived when little Arthur spoke
Of "Papa Philip!" and his balmy kiss
Renewed lost yearnings for a father's bliss.
And something glittered in the boy's bright hair:
I kissed him back, but turned away my head
To hide the pang I would not have thee share,
Dear wife! from whom the dearest promise fled.
God cannot chide so sacred a despair,
But still I dream that somewhere there must be
The spirit of a child that waits for me.

And evening fell, and Arthur, rosy-limbed
And snowy-gowned, in human beauty sweet,
Came pattering up with little naked feet
To kiss the good-night cup, that overbrimmed
With love two fathers and two mothers gave.
The steady rain against the windows drave,
And round the house the noises of the night
Mixed in a lulling music: dry old wood

Burned on the hearth in leaps of ruddy light,
And on the table purple beakers stood
Of harmless wine, from grapes that ripened on
The sunniest hill-sides of the smooth Garonne.
When Arthur slept, and doors were closed, and we
Sat folded in a sweeter privacy
Than even the secret-loving moon bestows,
Spoke Ernest: "Edith, shall I read the rest?"
She, while the spirit of a happy rose
Visited her cheeks, consenting smiled, and pressed
The hand he gave. "With what I now shall read,"
He added, "Philip, you must be content.
No further runs my journal, nor, indeed,
Beyond this chapter is there further need;
Because the gift of Song was chiefly lent
To give consoling music for the joys
We lack, and not for those which we possess:
I now no longer need that gift, to bless
My heart, — *your* heart, my Edith, and your boy's!"

Therewith he read: the fingers of the rain
In light staccatos on the window played,
Mixed with the flame's contented hum, and made
Low harmonies to suit the varied strain.

THE RETURN OF SPRING.

Have I passed through Death's unconscious birth,
  In a dream the midnight bare?
I look on another and fairer Earth:
  I breathe a wondrous air!

A spirit of beauty walks the hills,
  A spirit of love the plain;
The shadows are bright, and the sunshine fills
  The air with a diamond rain!

Before my vision the glories swim,
  To the dance of a tune unheard:
Is an angel singing where woods are dim,
  Or is it an amorous bird?

Is it a spike of azure flowers,
  Deep in the meadows seen,
Or is it the peacock's neck, that towers
  Out of the spangled green?

Is a white dove glancing across the blue,
  Or an opal taking wing?
For my soul is dazzled through and through,
  With the splendor of the Spring.

Is it she that shines, as never before,
  The tremulous hills above,—
Or the heart within me, awake once more
  To the dawning light of love?

MORNING.

Along the east, where late the dark impended,
A dusky gleam is born:
The watches of the night are ended,
And heaven foretells the morn!

The hills of home, no longer hurled together
In one wide blotch of night,
Lift up their heads through misty ether,
Distinct in rising light.

Then, after pangs of darkness slowly dying,
O'er the delivered world
Comes Morn, with every banner flying
And every sail unfurled!

So long the night, so chill, so blank and dreary,
I thought the sun was dead;
But yonder burn his beacons cheery
On peaks of cloudy red:

And yonder fly his scattered golden arrows,
  And smite the hills with day,
While Night her vain dominion narrows
  And westward wheels away.

A sweeter air revives the new creation,
  The dews are tears of bliss,
And Earth, in amorous palpitation,
  Receives her bridegroom's kiss.

Bathed in the morning, let my heart surrender
  The doubts that darkness gave,
And rise to meet the advancing splendor —
  O Night! no more thy slave.

I breathe at last, thy gloomy reign forgetting,
  Thy weary watches done,
Thy last pale star behind me setting,
  The freedom of the sun!

QUESTIONS.

One thought sits brooding in my bosom,
As broodeth in her nest the dove;
A strange, delicious doubt o'ercomes me, —
But is it love?

I see her, hear her, daily, nightly:
My secret dreams around her move,
Still nearer drawn in sweet attraction; —
Can this be love?

Is 't love without his tender tumult?
Or passion purified from pain?
In calmer forms the old emotions
Returned again?

So still the stream, towards her setting,
I whisper: Can it rise above
Her banks, and flood the guarded island
Where blooms her love?

Will she, to hear a voice so timid,
  A shy and doubtful heart incline,
Though desperate hope and endless longing
      Awake in mine?

I breathe but peace when she is near me, —
  A peace her absence takes away:
My heart commands her constant presence:
      Will hers obey?

THE VISION.

I.

She came, long absent from my side,
And absent from my dreams, she came,
The earthly and the heavenly bride,
In maiden beauty glorified:
She looked upon me, angel-eyed:
She called me by my name.

II.

But I, whose heart to meet her sprang
And shook the fragile house of dreams,
Stood, smitten with a guilty pang:
In other groves and temples rang
The songs that once for her I sang,
By woods and faery streams.

III.

Her eyes had power to lift my head,
  And, timorous as a truant child,
I met the sacred light they shed,
The light of heaven around her spread:
She read my face; no word she said:
  I only saw she smiled.

IV.

"Canst thou forgive me, Angel mine,"
  I cried; "that Love at last beguiled
My heart to build a second shrine?
See, still I kneel and weep at thine,
But I am human, thou divine!"
  Still silently she smiled.

V.

"Dost undivided worship claim,
  To keep thine altar undefiled?
Or must I bear thy tender blame,
And in thy pardon feel my shame,
Whene'er I breathe another name?
  She looked at me, and smiled.

VI.

“Speak, speak!” and then my tears came fast,
  My troubled heart with doubt grew wild:
“Will ’t vex the love, which still thou hast,
To know that I have peace at last?”
And from my dream the vision passed,
  And still, in passing, smiled.

LOVE RETURNED.

I.

He was a boy when first we met;
  His eyes were mixed of dew and fire,
And on his candid brow was set
  The sweetness of a chaste desire:
But in his veins the pulses beat
  Of passion, waiting for its wing,
As ardent veins of summer heat
  Throb through the innocence of spring.

II.

As manhood came, his stature grew,
  And fiercer burned his restless eyes,
Until I trembled, as he drew
  From wedded hearts their young disguise.
Like wind-fed flame his ardor rose,
  And brought, like flame, a stormy rain:
In tumult, sweeter than repose,
  He tossed the souls of joy and pain.

III.

So many years of absence change!
  I knew him not when he returned:
His step was slow, his brow was strange,
  His quiet eye no longer burned.
When at my heart I heard his knock,
  No voice within his right confessed:
I could not venture to unlock
  Its chambers to an alien guest.

IV.

Then, at the threshold, spent and worn
  With fruitless travel, down he lay:
And I beheld the gleams of morn
  On his reviving beauty play.
I knelt, and kissed his holy lips,
  I washed his feet with pious care;
And from my life the long eclipse
  Drew off, and left his sunshine there.

V.

He burns no more with youthful fire;
  He melts no more in foolish tears;

Serene and sweet, his eyes inspire
  The steady faith of balanced years.
His folded wings no longer thrill,
  But in some peaceful flight of prayer :
He nestles in my heart so still,
  I scarcely feel his presence there.

VI.

O Love, that stern probation o'er,
  Thy calmer blessing is secure!
Thy beauteous feet shall stray no more,
  Thy peace and patience shall endure!
The lightest wind deflowers the rose,
  The rainbow with the sun departs,
But thou art centred in repose,
  And rooted in my heart of hearts!

LOVE JUSTIFIED.

WITHIN my heart 't is clear at last:
  The haunting doubt in peace is laid,
Of faithlessness towards the Past,
  Which made reviving love afraid.

For Love in abnegation lives;
  His eye no sacrifice can dim;
He most is blessed when he gives
  A greater bliss than comes to him;

And true to him is true to all
  Whose brows are worth his crown to wear.
His chosen are not those who fall,
  Through loss of him, to blank despair,

But those whom he has left awhile,
  That in the dark their faith be tried, —
On whom his blessing yet shall smile,
  If in the dark their faith abide.

No treason in my love I see,
  For treason cannot dwell with truth ·
But later blossoms crown a tree
  Too deeply set to die in youth.

The blighted promise of the old
  In this new love is reconciled;
For, when my heart confessed its hold,
  The lips of ancient sorrow smiled!

It brightens backward through the Past
  And gilds the gloomy path I trod,
And forward, till it fades at last
  In light, before the feet of God,

Where stands the saint, whose radiant brow
  This solace beams, while I adore:
Be happy: if thou lovedst not now,
  Thou never couldst have loved before!

A WOMAN.

I.

She is a woman: therefore, I a man,
  In so much as I love her. Could I more,
Then I were more a man. Our natures ran
  Together, brimming full, not flooding o'er
The banks of life, and evermore will run
In one full stream until our days are done.

II.

She is a woman, but of spirit brave
  To bear the loss of girlhood's giddy dreams;
The regal mistress, not the yielding slave
  Of her ideal, spurning that which seems
For that which is, and, as her fancies fall,
Smiling: the truth of love outweighs them all.

III.

She looks through life, and with a balance just
Weighs men and things, beholding as they are
The lives of others: in the common dust
She finds the fragments of the ruined star:
Proud, with a pride all feminine and sweet,
No path can soil the whiteness of her feet.

IV.

The steady candor of her gentle eyes
Strikes dead deceit, laughs vanity away;
She hath no room for petty jealousies,
Where Faith and Love divide their tender sway.
Of either sex she owns the nobler part:
Man's honest brow and woman's faithful heart.

V.

She is a woman, who, if Love were guide,
Would climb to power, or in obscure content
Sit down: accepting fate with changeless pride,—
A reed in calm, in storm a staff unbent:
No pretty plaything, ignorant of life,
But Man's true mother, and his equal wife.

THE COUNT OF GLEICHEN.

I READ that story of the Saxon knight,
  Who, leaving spouse and feudal fortress, made
The Cross of Christ his guerdon in the fight,
  And joined the last Crusade:

Whom, in the chase on Damietta's sands
  Estrayed, the Saracens in ambush caught,
And unto Cairo, to the Soldan's hands,
  A wretched captive brought:

Whom then the Soldan's child, a damsel brave,
  Saw, pitied, comforted, and made him free,
And with him fled, herself a willing slave
  In Love's captivity.

I read how he to bless her love was fain,
  To whom his renovated life he owed,
Yet with a pang the towers beheld again
  Where still his wife abode:

The wife whom first he loved: would she not scorn
The second bride he could not choose but wed,
The second mother to his children, born
In her divided bed?

Lo! at his castle's foot the noble dame
With tears of blessing, holy, undefiled
By human pain, received him when he came,
And kissed the Soldan's child!

My tears were on the pages as I read
The touching close: I made the story mine,
Within whose heart, long plighted to the dead,
Love built his living shrine.

I too had dared, a captive in the land,
To pay with love the love that broke my chain:
Would she, who waited, stretch the pardoning hand,
When I returned again?

Would she, my freedom and my bliss to know,
With my disloyalty be reconciled,
And from her bower in Eden look below,
And bless the Soldan's child?

For she is lost: but she, the later bride,
  Who came my ruined fortune to restore,
Back from the desert wanders at my side,
  And leads me home once more.

If human love, she sighs, could move a wife
  The holiest sacrifice of love to make,
Then the transfigured angel of thy life
  Is happier for thy sake!

BEFORE THE BRIDAL.

Now the night is overpast,
  And the mist is cleared away:
On my barren life at last
  Breaks the bright, reluctant day.

Day of payment for the wrong
  I was doomed so long to bear;
Day of promise, day of song,
  Day that makes the future fair!

Let me wake to bliss alone:
  Let me bury every fear:
What I prayed for, is my own;
  What was distant, now is near.

For the happy hour that waits
  No reproachful shade shall bring,
And I hear forgiving Fates
  In the happy bells that ring.

Leave the song that now is mute,
  For the sweeter song begun:
Leave the blossom for the fruit,
  And the rainbow for the sun!

POSSESSION.

I.

" It was our wedding-day
A month ago," dear heart, I hear you say.
If months, or years, or ages since have passed,
I know not: I have ceased to question Time.
I only know that once there pealed a chime
Of joyous bells, and then I held you fast,
And all stood back, and none my right denied,
And forth we walked: the world was free and wide
Before us. Since that day
I count my life: the Past is washed away.

II.

It was no dream, that vow:
It was the voice that woke me from a dream, —
A happy dream, I think; but I am waking now,
And drink the splendor of a sun supreme
That turns the mist of former tears to gold.
Within these arms I hold

The fleeting promise, chased so long in vain:
Ah, weary bird! thou wilt not fly again:
Thy wings are clipped, thou canst no more depart, —
Thy nest is builded in my heart!

III.

I was the crescent; thou
The silver phantom of the perfect sphere,
Held in its bosom: in one glory now
Our lives united shine, and many a year —
Not the sweet moon of bridal only — we
One lustre, ever at the full, shall be:
One pure and rounded light, one planet whole,
One life developed, one completed soul!
For I in thee, and thou in me,
Unite our cloven halves of destiny.

IV.

God knew His chosen time:
He bade me slowly ripen to my prime,
And from my boughs withheld the promised fruit,
Till storm and sun gave vigor to the root.
Secure, O Love! secure
Thy blessing is: I have thee day and night:
Thou art become my blood, my life, my light:
God's mercy thou, and therefore shalt endure!

UNDER THE MOON.

I.

From you and home I sleep afar,
Under the light of a lonely star,
Under the moon that marvels why
Away from you and home I lie.
Ah! love no language can declare,
The hovering warmth, the tender care,
The yielding, sweet, invisible air
That clasps your bosom, and fans your cheek
With the breath of words I cannot speak,—
Such love I give, such warmth impart:
The fragrance of a blossomed heart.

II.

The moon looks in upon my bed,
Her yearning glory rays my head,
And round me clings, a lonely light,
The aureole of the winter night;
But in my heart a gentle pain,
A balmier splendor in my brain,

Lead me beyond the frosty plane, —
Lead me afar, to mellower skies,
Where under the moon a palace lies;
Where under the moon our bed is made,
Half in splendor and half in shade.

III.

The marble flags of the corridor
Through open windows meet the floor,
And Moorish arches in darkness rise
Against the gleam of the silver skies:
Beyond, in flakes of starry light,
A fountain prattles to the night,
And dusky cypresses, withdrawn
In silent conclave, stud the lawn;
While mystic woodlands, more remote,
In seas of airy silver float,
So hung in heaven, the stars that set
Seem glossy leaves the dew has wet
On topmost boughs, and sparkling yet.

IV.

In from the terraced garden blows
The spicy soul of the tuberose,

As if 't were the odor of strains that pour
From the nightingale's throat as never before;
For he sings not now of wounding thorn,
He sings as the lark in the golden morn, —
A song of joy, a song of bliss,
Passionate notes that clasp and kiss,
Perfect peace and perfect pride,
Love rewarded and satisfied,
For I see you, darling, at my side.

V.

I see you, darling, at my side:
I clasp you closer, in sacred pride.
I shut my eyes, my senses fail,
Becalmed by Night's ambrosial gale.
Softer than dews the planets weep,
  Descends a sweeter peace than sleep;
All wandering sounds and motions die
  In the silent glory of the sky;
But, as the moon goes down the West,
Your heart, against my happy breast,
Says in its beating: Love is Rest.

THE MYSTIC SUMMER.

'T IS not the dropping of the flower,
  The blush of fruit upon the tree,
Though Summer ripens, hour by hour,
  The garden's sweet maternity:

'T is not that birds have ceased to build,
  And wait their brood with tender care;
That corn is golden in the field,
  And clover balm is in the air; —

Not these the season's splendor bring,
  And crowd with life the happy year,
Nor yet, where yonder fountains sing,
  The blaze of sunshine, hot and clear.

In thy full womb, O Summer! lies
  A secret hope, a joy unsung,
Held in the hush of these calm skies,
  And trembling on the forest's tongue.

The lands of harvest throb anew
  In shining pulses, far away;
The Night distils a dearer dew,
  And sweeter eyelids has the Day.

And not in vain the peony burns,
  In bursting globes, her crimson fire,
Her incense-dropping ivory urns
  The lily lifts in many a spire:

And not in vain the tulips clash
  In revelry the cups they hold
Of fiery wine, until they dash
  With ruby streaks the splendid gold!

Send down your roots the mystic charm
  That warms and flushes all your flowers,
And with the summer's touch disarm
  The thraldom of the under powers,

Until, in caverns, buried deep,
  Strange fragrance reach the diamond's home,
And murmurs of the garden sweep
  The houses of the frighted gnome!

For, piercing through their black repose,
  And shooting up beyond the sun,
I see that Tree of Life, which rose
  Before the eyes of Solomon:

Its boughs, that, in the light of God,
  Their bright, innumerous leaves display, —
Whose hum of life is borne abroad
  By winds that shake the dead away.

And, trembling on a branch afar,
  The topmost nursling of the skies,
I see my bud, the fairest star
  That ever dawned for watching eyes.

Unnoticed on the boundless tree,
  Its fragrant promise fills the air;
Its little bell expands, for me,
  A tent of silver, lily-fair.

All life to that one centre tends ;
  All joy and beauty thence outflow ;
Her sweetest gifts the summer spends,
  To teach that sweeter bud to blow.

So, compassed by the vision's gleam,
  In trembling hope, from day to day,
As in some bright, bewildering dream,
  The mystic summer wanes away.

A WATCH OF THE NIGHT.

Blow, winds of midnight, blow!
The clouds, fast-flying, chase
Across the pallid face
Of yonder moon, and go!

Sweep, as ye list, the land:
Hurl down the heavy corn,
And wrench the trees forlorn
That struggle where they stand!

Though mighty to destroy,
To me ye bring no fear;
But in your voice I hear
An echo of my joy.

Life — life to me ye bring:
The precious soul, that takes
Its life from mine, awakes,
And soon will crown me king.

I stand with silent breath,
To hear one little cry
Ring through the roaring sky,
And worlds of Life and Death.

Wake, timid soul, and be!
Two Fathers wait thy birth:
The love of Heaven and Earth
Stands by to welcome thee!

THE FATHER.

THE fateful hour, when Death stood by
  And stretched his threatening hand in vain,
Is over now, and Life's first cry
  Speaks feeble triumph through its pain.

But yesterday, and thee the Earth
  Inscribed not on her mighty scroll:
To-day she opes the gate of birth,
  And gives the spheres another soul.

But yesterday, no fruit from me
  The rising winds of Time had hurled:
To-day, a father, — can it be
  A child of mine is in the world?

I look upon the little frame,
  As helpless on my arm it lies:
Thou giv'st me, child, a father's name,
  God's earliest name in Paradise.

Like Him, creator too I stand :
His Power and Mystery seem more near ;
Thou giv'st me honor in the land,
And giv'st my life duration here.

But love, to-day, is more than pride ;
Love sees his star of triumph shine,
For Life nor Death can now divide
The souls that wedded breathe in thine :

Mine and thy mother's, whence arose
The copy of my face in thee ;
And as thine eyelids first unclose,
My own young eyes look up to me.

Look on me, child, once more, once more,
Even with those weak, unconscious eyes ;
Stretch the small hands that help implore ;
Salute me with thy wailing cries !

This is the blessing and the prayer
A father's sacred place demands :
Ordain me, darling, for thy care,
And lead me with thy helpless hands !

THE MOTHER.

Paler, and yet a thousand times more fair
  Than in thy girlhood's freshest bloom, art thou:
A softer sun-flush tints thy golden hair,
  A sweeter grace adorns thy gentle brow.

Lips that shall call thee "mother!" at thy breast
  Feed the young life, wherein thy nature feels
Its dear fulfilment: little hands are pressed
  On the white fountain Love alone unseals.

Look down, and let Life's tender daybreak throw
  A second radiance on thy ripened hour:
Retrace thine own forgotten advent so,
  And in the bud behold thy perfect flower.

Nay, question not: whatever lies beyond
  God will dispose. Sit thus, Madonna mine,
For thou art haloed with a love as fond
  As Jewish Mary gave the Child Divine.

I lay my own proud title at thy feet;
  Thine the first, holiest right to love shalt be:
Though in his heart our wedded pulses beat,
  His sweetest life our darling draws from thee.

The father in his child beholds this truth,
  His perfect manhood has assumed its reign:
Thou wear'st anew the roses of thy youth, —
  The mother in her child is born again.

THE FAMILY.

DEAR Love, whatever fate
  The flying years unfold,
There 's none can dissipate
  The happiness we hold.
Whatever cloud may rise,
  The very storms grow mild
Where bend the blissful skies
  O'er Husband, Wife, and Child.

The errant dreams that failed,
  The promises that fled,
The roseate hopes that paled,
  The loves that now are dead,
The treason of the Past, —
  All, all are reconciled:
Life's glory shines at last
  On Father, Mother, Child!

To meet the days and years,
  With hands that never part;
To shed no secret tears,
  To hide no lonely heart:
To know our longing stilled,
  To feel that God has smiled:
These are the dreams fulfilled
  In Husband, Wife, and Child, —
  In Father, Mother, Child!

Thus came the Poet's Journal to an end.
His heart's completed music ceased to flow
From Ernest's lips: the tale I wished to know
Was wholly mine. "I am content, dear friend,"
I said: "to me no voice can be obscure
Wherein your nature speaks: the chords I hear,
Too far and frail to strike a stranger's ear."
With that, I bowed to Edith's forehead pure,
And kissed her with a brother's blameless kiss:
"To you the fortune of these days I owe,
My other Ernest, like him most in this,
That you can hear the cries of ancient woe
With holy pity, free from any blame
Of jealous love, and find your highest bliss
To know, through you his life's fulfilment came."
"And through him, mine," the woman's heart replied;
For Love's humility is Love's true pride.

"These are your sweetest poems, and your best,"
To him I said. "I know not," answered he,
"They are my truest. I have ceased to be
The ambitious knight of Song, that shook his crest

In public tilts: the sober hermit I,
Whose evening songs but few approach to hear, —
Who, if those few should cease to lend an ear,
Would sing them to the forest and the sky
Contented: singing for myself alone.
No fear that any poet dies unknown,
Whose songs are written in the hearts that know
And love him, though their partial verdict show
The tenderness that moves the critic's blame.
Those few have power to lift his name above
Forgetfulness, to grant that noblest fame
Which sets its trumpet to the lips of Love!"

"Nay, then," said I, "you are already crowned.
If your ambition in the loving pride
Of us, your friends, is cheaply satisfied,
We are those trumpets: do you hear them sound?"
And Edith smilingly together wound
Light stems of ivy to a garland fair,
And pressed it archly on her husband's hair;
But he, with earnest voice, though in his eyes
A happy laughter shone, protesting, said:
"Respect, dear friends, the Muse's sanctities,
Nor mock, with wreaths upon a living head,
The holy laurels of the deathless Dead.
Crown Love, crown Truth when first her brow appears,

And crown the Hero when his deeds are done:
The Poet's leaves are gathered, one by one,
In the slow process of the doubtful years.
Who seeks too eagerly, he shall not find:
Who, seeking not, pursues with single mind
Art's lofty aim, to him will she accord,
At her appointed time, the sure reward."

The tall clock, standing sentry in the hall,
Struck midnight: on the panes no longer beat
The weary storm: the wind began to fall,
And through the breaking darkness glimmered, sweet
With tender stars, the flying gleams of sky.
" Come, Edith, lend your voice to crown the night,
And give the new day sunny break," said I:
She, listening first in self-deceiving plight
Of young maternal trouble, for a cry
From Arthur's crib, sat down in happy calm,
And sang to Ernest's heart his own thanksgiving psalm:

Thou who sendest sun and rain,
Thou who spendest bliss and pain,
Good with bounteous hand bestowing,
Evil for Thy will allowing,—
Though Thy ways we cannot see,
All is just that comes from Thee.

In the peace of hearts at rest,
In the child at mother's breast,
In the lives that now surround us,
In the deaths that sorely wound us,
Though we may not understand,
Father, we behold Thy hand!

Hear the happy hymn we raise;
Take the love which is Thy praise;
Give content in each condition:
Bend our hearts in sweet submission,
And Thy trusting children prove
Worthy of the Father's love!

PASSING THE SIRENS.

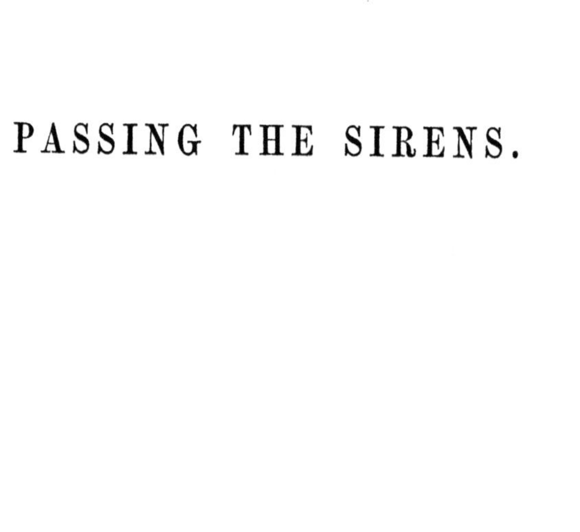

PASSING THE SIRENS.

ULYSSES.

THE headlands pale, the long, far-pointing cliffs
Of Circe's isle, are fading on the sea.
Our oars are idle, for the rising wind,
Strong Auster, fills the sail: the galley's beak
From every billow tears the garland foam,
And trails the scattered sea-blooms in her wake.
We should be near the islands: look, my men,
You, Perimedes, look, whose hawk-eyes peer,
Deep-set, beneath their many-wrinkled lids,
Tell me if yon be shores which rather float
On the unburdened seas, the isles of heat,
Delusive vapor-lands that come and go,
Than rise from under, lifting solid fronts
To meet the turmoil of the changing tides.

A steady helm, my pilot! yonder lies
The broader channel: look not on the shores
That glimmering change from purple into green,
But mark the burning highway of the sun,

Now to his bath descending, — follow that,
Straight through, and out on waters unexplored,
Ay, though we reach the Thunder's awful house,
The caverned hell of storms, than once touch keel
In these smooth harbors. Turn away your eyes,
My sailors, from the fair, fast-rising isles,
That drug the winds with many a musky flower
To sleep, that smooth the waters as with oil,
And open bowery laps of sunny coves,
To tempt your tempest-battered frames. And me,
Who never gave ye toils I did not share,
Or tasted pleasures I denied ye, — who
In Chian ports the flaccid wine-skin filled,
And in the arms of soft Ionian girls
Ye after storms long anchorage allowed, —
Me bind ye fast, here, at the mainmast's foot,
And stop my ears with wool, lest I should lose
The settled will that drives my purpose on,
And falter with slack sails, the shame of all,
Of ye, my men, and all who honored me,
Heroes and demigods, in Troy. For I,
Wiser than ye in scheming, stronger proved
In much endurance, have the keener sense
Of all delights and all indulgences,
The more temptation to forbidden lusts.
Let me not hear the singing from the isles,

Or see the Sirens, naked in the shade,
Spread their alluring couches!

Ye, who toiled
With me, whom now from Circe's sty I saved,
Whose fate and mine is one, hear these my words:
Brail up the slackened mainsail to the yard:
Strong Auster fails: in order sit ye down,
Each on his bench, within the hollow ship,
And smite the billows of the hoary sea!
Let the white blades of fir keep even time,
Rattling together, — nor the helmsman fall
A hair's breadth from his course. It comes at last!
Whate'er you hear, the tasks I set perform
In order! Press the stoppers of my ears:
Nay, stop your own, — your faces grow too keen, —
Your eyes are full of wild and hungry light.
Now, by Poseidon! my right arm is free,
Look shoreward, and I slay you! Orpheus, there,
Tightens the loose chords of his lyre: he leans
Against the spray-wet altar on the prow,
Gazing straight forward, as his soul were dropt
Into the ocean of the golden sky.
Ay, sing, and overtake it with your song,
And if the Sirens not more rugged be
Than pines of Thessaly, that left the hills

To hear your music, they will quit their isles,
Shorn of their spells, your captives, following us
In dumb subjection through the barren seas.

THE SIRENS.

They are rough with the salt of the sea,
  They are brown with the brand of the sun:
They are weary, weary of the sea;
  They are weary of the sun.
Tug at the heavy oar;
Heave at the stubborn sail, —
Tossed in the mid-sea gale,
Wrecked on the fatal shore!

Here in our isles is rest,
  Here there is rest alone:
Sweet is rest, ah, sweet is rest,
White the arms and warm the breast, —
Naught beyond but the unknown West,
  Naught but the waves unknown!

From their foreheads wipe the brine,
Round their brows the poppies twine:
Lay them on couches of balmy thyme,
Deep in the shade of the bee-loved lime!

Let them sleep: the restless deep
Here no more compels to keep
The weary watches that baffle sleep:
Toil is here a thing unknown,
  Peril is a stranger here;
Sweetest rest, and rest alone,
  Waits the weary mariner.

ORPHEUS.

You sit serene upon your golden seats,
In the bright climate of eternal calm.
No pain can touch you, and the tumult raised
By foolish men dies in this lower air:
But Song — when from the Poet's perfect lips
Divinest song is shed — finds entrance there,
And bears his message even to your board.
Great Zeus lifts up his awful brow: his beard
Drops from its knotted coils, and sweeps his knees;
The thunder's edge grows keener in his grasp.
And the grave pleasure seated in his eyes
Brightens Olympian ether. Pallas hears;
Her brow's chill adamant is less severe:
And large-eyed Herè lifts the violet lids,
Shading the languid fountains of her eyes,
To look the joy her indolence makes dumb.

You hear me, Gods! you hear and comfort me.
I see thee, whom in Delos I adored,
And unto whom, beyond the Thracian strait,
I built an altar on the windy isle
Beside the Tauric seas. Thy splendid hair,
Spread by the swiftness of thy chariot-wheels,
Rays with celestial gold thy forehead's arch,
And thine immortal lips, too sweet for man,
Too eloquent for woman, half unclose,
Unuttered consolation in their smile, —
Unspoken promises, whence hope is born
Of something happier, somewhere in the spheres.

THE SIRENS.

You have toiled enough, mariners!
  Labor no more:
Lower the canvas,
  Leave the oar:
Over our island
  Storms cannot come:
Winds are in slumber:
  Thunder is dumb.
Only the nightingale
  Sings in her nest:
Balmy our couches,

Come to your rest!
Roses shall garland you,
Arms shall encircle you,
Lips shall be pressed!
Wine in the goblets
Shines ruby and gold, —
Strength to the weary,
Warmth to the cold,
Blood to the wasted,
Youth to the old!
Ah, and the rapture
Thousandfold dearer,
Ne'er to be told:
Learn ye the secret, —
Taste ye the sweetness, —
Beauty's possession
Belongs to the bold!

ORPHEUS.

Not Minos, iron judge, alone shall speak
Our final sentence; but the balance hangs,
Even while we live, in sight of all the Gods.
Our fates are weighed, and less unequal seem
To calm Olympian eyes, than ours, obscured
By films inseparate from this cloudy earth.

As one who, sitting on the high-prowed ship,
Sees not the rosy splendor of the sail
At morning, when, a planet of the sea,
It shines afar to dwellers on the land;
So we the later radiance of our lives,
Now shining, see not. We have toiled, 't is true:
Stared Danger's lion boldly in the face
Until he turned: borne wounds and racking pains;
The frosts of Colchian winters, and the fire
That darts from Cancer on the Libyan shore:
Brief joy, brief rest, stern labor, suffering,
Are ours, — yet have we kept, as heroes should,
The steady cheerfulness of temperate hearts,
Courage, and mutual trust. We shall not leave
The vapid dust of idlers in our urns:
Behind our lives shall burn the shining tracks
Of splendid deeds, and men long after us
Shall build the steadfast mansion of our fame.
What here we lose, shall be our portion there
Among the Happy Fields, — divine repose
Eternally prolonged, and blameless joy.
We in that larger freedom of the blest
Heroic shades, shall find our chosen seats.
This restless life beneath the hollow sky,
And looking o'er the edges of the world
Far from the anchored shores, the tongues of air,

The doubtful voices heard in sounding caves
Where gods abide, dim whispers, teaching us,
God-like, the secrets of the elements,
Have smoothed our entrance to the ample realms
Where Youth returns, and Joy, so timorous now,
Drops, like a weary dove, to fly no more.

THE SIRENS.

Listen, ye mariners! hark to our promises!
  Prouder than pleasure the gifts we confer:
Though unto passion the Siren gives passion,
  He who seeks power receives it from her!

Labor no longer, confronting the turbulent
  Elements, ever opposing your will:
Secrets we know, knowing all things, immortal, —
  Equal with gods your desires to fulfil.

Secrets that chain in his caverns the Thunder,
  Fetter the winds when they eagerest are:
Loosen the stream from its urns in the mountain,
  Ay, and the vaults of the earthquake unbar!

Come, and the delicate spell shall be spoken,
  Subtly to seize, and securely to bind, —
Wisdom and eloquence, honeyed persuasion,
  Giving ye mastery over your kind.

Men shall adore ye, and even Immortals
  Stoop from their thrones in Olympian flame:
All that have conquered and triumphed before ye
  Dust shall become at the feet of your fame!

ULYSSES.

It cleaves the muffled sense; it penetrates
The guarded porches of the brain, no lance
Hurled from a giant's arm more sure: it hums
And stings within me, as the brown bee hums,
Shut in the folded heart of some rich flower,
Drinking its drop of honey, — so it creeps
Within the purple blossom of my heart,
That music: and the very thrills of fear
To hide the secret honey of my lust,
Aid the seduction and betray the spoil.
You see me tremble: will it never cease?
It follows, follows, clearer as we pass
The channel's throat, the final isles abeam,
And sweeter, keener, more alluring still,
From looking on the unfriendly seas. My men,
Sing me your loudest songs — the yo-heave-O!
Of Aulis, or the coarse carousal-glees
Of Tenedos and Troy! What? are ye dumb,
With eyes that burn like half-extinguished brands,
Fanned with desires new-blown, and mutinous

With thought of coming peril? Nay, then, shout!
Yell with the rage of disappointed lust,
The spite of thwarted opportunity,
The frenzy which an unrelenting Fate
Smiles at, and so increases! Curse your chief,
Even me, Ulysses, — lash yourselves to wrath,
Like Satyrs when the Bacchic madness takes
Autumnal hills, so ye but overcome
That still-pursuing music! Bravely done!
My heart is tougher for that brawny roar,
Which, in the old time heard, could always turn
The battle's doubtful scale.

A fresher wind
Foreruns the presence of the rearward night;
Salt scud flies over us, and pale sea-fire
Flashes around the rudder. Set me free:
I am your captain, — you are still my men;
My sailors, whose obedience makes me strong,
My comrades, whom I love. See! yonder sinks
The glimmering beach astern: the songs are still;
The lovely Treachery withdraws at last
Its baffled spells. Now, whatsoever waits
For us, of new adventure, hostile winds,
Deceitful reefs, leagues of unharbored shore,
Or combats with strange tribes, gigantic forms
Cyclopean, or of bestial shape abhorred,

The worst is passed: and ye have proved to-day
Strong to resist, where mere resistance counts
Above all courage to confront the shocks
Whereon true manly steel but rings unharmed;
But this assails us from the softer side,
Melting the hero's marrow. Wherefore, now,
Broach we that skin of amber Cretan wine,
First pouring, as is meet, libations large
To Pallas, and Poseidon, and to Zeus.
Ho, Orpheus! Are you dreaming on the prow?
Or have the Sirens through your trancèd ears
Rapt forth your soul? You cannot hear them now:
Come down: our hearts need festal music. Sing
As when we skirted Delos, and the white
Uplifted temple shone like morning snow,
'Twixt the blue hemispheres of sky and sea!

ORPHEUS.

I looked on him whose marble mansion gleams
High over Delos, — did the Sirens sing?
Who hears their music, sitting in the light
Of his immortal features, breathing balm
Shook from the rich confusion of his curls?
He gave me entrance to the happy meads
Beyond the rainbow's span: I breathed, with him,

The perfect ether of Olympian skies:
I heard the piercing sweetness of his lyre
Strike harmony through all the shuddering heart
Of Chaos, while from blissful stars that slid,
Sparkling, around him, in their crystal grooves,
Sweet noises came, responsive. I beheld
His music shape the world's eternal law.
Immortal Justice there was justified:
Fate span an equal thread: more vile became
Rebellion to the gods, obedience light,
Complaint unworthy. They the soonest reach
The shining fields where shades of heroes walk,
Who, spurning passion, rise with even souls
O'er this, your madness, as an eagle hangs
Above the thunder, in the sunshine poised.
Your voices call me from my lofty dream,
Yet think not that my spirit stoops to share
Your noisy gladness! Rather let me breathe
This pulse of music throbbing at my heart,
Until the speaking wires shall give me back
Some fragments of the voices of the Gods.

THE SAILORS.

No doubt you know the language of the Gods,
You, Orpheus, with your eyes that look afar,

Your ears, dumb to the thunder when you sing;
But you, our Captain, know the hearts of men.
Here, pour this cup of amber wine to Zeus,
This, to Poseidon, — this, to Pallas, — this
Drink, shipmates, to Ulysses, from your hearts!
Sing, Orpheus, if you like: we do not want
Your Samothracian songs that cheat our ears
Like wind among the pines, — but lusty staves,
"*Down with the Dardans!*" or "*The Girl of Cos,*"
Songs that our captain loves: we sing with him.
Who knows us, suffers with us, feels for us,
Stands at the post of peril at our head,
Strong to subdue our hot, rebellious blood,
Free to forgive the easy vice, because
He feels it tugging at his heart the same, —
Him will we follow, though ten thousand isles
Of Sirens tempted, to the utmost verge
Where Earth falls sheer away, and under where
The great sun rolls, and the stars hide at dawn.
Drink with us, Captain! strike hands once again!
We swear anew the obedient oath we took
When first you shipped us, wild, wayfaring knaves,
Among the scattered isles. The watch is set;
The night is fortunate; the wind is fair;
Our hearts are happy, — let our compact hold!

VARIOUS POEMS.

PORPHYROGENITUS.

I.

Born in the purple! born in the purple!
    Heir to the sceptre and crown!
Lord over millions and millions of vassals, —
    Monarch of mighty renown!
Where, do you ask, are my banner-proud castles?
    Where my imperial town?

II.

Where are the ranks of my far-flashing lances, —
    Trumpets, courageous of sound, —
Galloping squadrons and rocking armadas,
    Guarding my kingdom around?
Where are the pillars that blazon my borders,
    Threatening the alien ground?

III.

Vainly you ask, if you wear not the purple,
    Sceptre and diadem own;
Ruling, yourself, over prosperous regions,
    Seated supreme on your throne.
Subjects have nothing to give but allegiance:
    Monarchs meet monarchs alone.

IV.

But, if a king, you shall stand on my ramparts,
    Look on the lands that I sway,
Number the domes of magnificent cities,
    Shining in valleys away, —
Number the mountains whose foreheads are golden,
    Lakes that are azure with day.

V.

Whence I inherited such a dominion?
    What was my forefathers' line?
Homer and Sophocles, Pindar and Sappho,
    First were anointed divine:
Theirs were the realms that a god might have governed,
    Ah, and how little is mine!

VI.

Hafiz in Orient shared with Petrarca
  Thrones of the East and the West;
Shakespeare succeeded to limitless empire,
  Greatest of monarchs, and best:
Few of his children inherited kingdoms,
  Provinces only, the rest.

VII.

Keats has his vineyards, and Shelley his islands;
  Coleridge in Xanadu reigns;
Wordsworth is eyried aloft on the mountains,
  Goethe has mountains and plains;
Yet, though the world has been parcelled among them,
  A world to be parcelled remains.

VIII.

Blessing enough to be born in the purple,
  Though but a monarch in name, —
Though in the desert my palace is builded,
  Far from the highways of Fame:
Up with my standards! salute me with trumpets!
  Crown me with regal acclaim!

THE SONG OF THE CAMP.

"GIVE us a song!" the soldiers cried,
The outer trenches guarding,
When the heated guns of the camps allied
Grew weary of bombarding.

The dark Redan, in silent scoff,
Lay, grim and threatening, under;
And the tawny mound of the Malakoff
No longer belched its thunder.

There was a pause. A guardsman said:
"We storm the forts to-morrow;
Sing while we may, another day
Will bring enough of sorrow."

They lay along the battery's side,
Below the smoking cannon:
Brave hearts, from Severn and from Clyde,
And from the banks of Shannon.

They sang of love, and not of fame;
  Forgot was Britain's glory:
Each heart recalled a different name,
  But all sang "Annie Lawrie."

Voice after voice caught up the song,
  Until its tender passion
Rose like an anthem, rich and strong, —
  Their battle-eve confession.

Dear girl, her name he dared not speak,
  But, as the song grew louder,
Something upon the soldier's cheek
  Washed off the stains of powder.

Beyond the darkening ocean burned
  The bloody sunset's embers,
While the Crimean valleys learned
  How English love remembers.

And once again a fire of hell
  Rained on the Russian quarters,
With scream of shot, and burst of shell,
  And bellowing of the mortars!

And Irish Nora's eyes are dim
  For a singer, dumb and gory;
And English Mary mourns for him
  Who sang of "Annie Lawrie."

Sleep, soldiers! still in honored rest
  Your truth and valor wearing:
The bravest are the tenderest, —
  The loving are the daring.

THE VINEYARD-SAINT.

She, pacing down the vineyard walks,
  Put back the branches, one by one,
Stripped the dry foliage from the stalks,
  And gave their bunches to the sun.

On fairer hill-sides, looking south,
  The vines were brown with cankerous rust,
The earth was hot with summer drouth,
  And all the grapes were dim with dust.

Yet here some blessed influence rained
  From kinder skies, the season through;
On every bunch the bloom remained,
  And every leaf was washed in dew.

I saw her blue eyes, clear and calm;
  I saw the aureole of her hair;
I heard her chant some unknown psalm,
  In triumph half, and half in prayer.

"Hail, maiden of the vines!" I cried:
  "Hail, Oread of the purple hill!
For vineyard fauns too fair a bride,
  For me thy cup of welcome fill!

Unlatch the wicket; let me in,
  And, sharing, make thy toil more dear:
No riper vintage holds the bin
  Than that our feet shall trample here.

"Beneath thy beauty's light I glow,
  As in the sun those grapes of thine:
Touch thou my heart with love, and lo!
  The foaming must is turned to wine!"

She, pausing, stayed her careful task,
  And, lifting eyes of steady ray,
Blew, as a wind the mountain's mask
  Of mist, my cloudy words away.

No troubled flush o'erran her cheek;
  But when her quiet lips did stir,
My heart knelt down to hear her speak,
  And mine the blush I sought in her.

" O, not for me," she said, " the vow
 So lightly breathed, to break erelong ;
The vintage-garland on the brow ;
 The revels of the dancing throng !

" To maiden love I shut my heart,
 Yet none the less a stainless bride ;
I work alone, I dwell apart,
 Because my work is sanctified.

" A virgin hand must tend the vine,
 By virgin feet the vat be trod,
Whose consecrated gush of wine
 Becomes the blessed blood of God !

" No sinful purple here shall stain,
 Nor juice profane these grapes afford ;
But reverent lips their sweetness drain
 Around the Table of the Lord.

" The cup I fill, of chaster gold,
 Upon the lighted altar stands ;
There, when the gates of heaven unfold,
 The priest exalts it in his hands.

" The censer yields adoring breath,
The awful anthem sinks and dies,
While God, who suffered life and death,
Renews His ancient sacrifice.

" O sacred garden of the vine !
And blessed she, ordained to press
God's chosen vintage, for the wine
Of pardon and of holiness ! "

ICARUS.

I.

Io triumphe! Lo, thy certain art,
My crafty sire, releases us at length!
False Minos now may knit his baffled brows,
And in the labyrinth by thee devised
His brutish horns in angry search may toss
The Minotaur, — but thou and I are free!
See where it lies, one dark spot on the breast
Of plains far-shining in the long-lost day,
Thy glory and our prison! Either hand
Crete, with her hoary mountains, olive-clad
In twinkling silver, 'twixt the vineyard rows,
Divides the glimmering seas. On Ida's top
The sun, discovering first an earthly throne,
Sits down in splendor: lucent vapors rise
From folded glens among the awaking hills,
Expand their hovering films, and touch, and spread
In airy planes beneath us, hearths of air
Whereon the Morning burns her hundred fires.

II.

Take thou thy way between the cloud and wave,
O Dædalus, my father, steering forth
To friendly Samos, or the Carian shore!
But me the spaces of the upper heaven
Attract, the height, the freedom, and the joy.
For now, from that dark treachery escaped,
And tasting power which was the lust of youth,
Whene'er the white blades of the sea-gull's wings
Flashed round the headland, or the barbèd files
Of cranes returning clanged across the sky,
No half-way flight, no errand incomplete
I purpose. Not, as once in dreams, with pain
I mount, with fear and huge exertion hold
Myself a moment, ere the sickening fall
Breaks in the shock of waking. Launched, at last,
Uplift on powerful wings, I veer and float
Past sunlit isles of cloud, that dot with light
The boundless archipelago of sky.
I fan the airy silence till it starts
In rustling whispers, swallowed up as soon;
I warm the chilly ether with my breath;
I with the beating of my heart make glad
The desert blue. Have I not raised myself
Unto this height, and shall I cease to soar?

The curious eagles wheel about my path:
With sharp and questioning eyes they stare at me,
With harsh, impatient screams they menace me,
Who, with these vans of cunning workmanship
Broad-spread, adventure on their high domain, —
Now mine, as well. Henceforth, ye clamorous birds,
I claim the azure empire of the air!
Henceforth I breast the current of the morn,
Between her crimson shores: a star, henceforth,
Upon the crawling dwellers of the earth
My forehead shines. The steam of sacred blood,
The smoke of burning flesh on altars laid,
Fumes of the temple-wine, and sprinkled myrrh,
Shall reach my palate ere they reach the Gods.

III.

Nay, am not I a God? What other wing,
If not a God's, could in the rounded sky
Hang thus in solitary poise? What need,
Ye proud Immortals, that my balanced plumes
Should grow, like yonder eagle's, from the nest?
It may be, ere my crafty father's line
Sprang from Erectheus, some artificer,
Who found you roaming wingless on the hills,
Naked, asserting godship in the dearth

Of loftier claimants, fashioned you the same.
Thence did you seize Olympus; thence your pride
Compelled the race of men, your slaves, to tear
The temple from the mountain's marble womb,
To carve you shapes more beautiful than they,
To sate your idle nostrils with the reek
Of gums and spices, heaped on jewelled gold.

IV

Lo, where Hyperion, through the glowing air
Approaching, drives! Fresh from his banquet-meats,
Flushed with Olympian nectar, angrily
He guides his fourfold span of furious steeds,
Convoyed by that bold Hour whose ardent torch
Burns up the dew, toward the narrow beach,
This long, projecting spit of cloudy gold
Whereon I wait to greet him when he comes.
Think not I fear thine anger: this day, thou,
Lord of the silver bow, shalt bring a guest
To sit in presence of the equal Gods
In your high hall: wheel but thy chariot near,
That I may mount beside thee!
—— What is this?
I hear the crackling hiss of singèd plumes!
The stench of burning feathers stifles me!

My loins are stung with drops of molten wax!—
Ai! ai! my ruined vans!—I fall! I die!

. . . . .

Ere the blue noon o'erspanned the bluer strait
Which parts Icaria from Samos, fell,
Amid the silent wonder of the air,
Fell with a shock that startled the still wave,
A shrivelled wreck of crisp, entangled plumes,
A head whence eagles' beaks had plucked the eyes,
And clots of wax, black limbs by eagles torn
In falling: and a circling eagle screamed
Around that floating horror of the sea
Derision, and above Hyperion shone.

THE BATH.

Off, fetters of the falser life, —
Weeds, that conceal the statue's form!
This silent world with truth is rife,
This wooing air is warm.

Now fall the thin disguises, planned
For men too weak to walk unblamed:
Naked beside the sea I stand, —
Naked, and not ashamed.

Where yonder dancing billows dip,
Far-off, to ocean's misty verge,
Ploughs Morning, like a full-sailed ship,
The Orient's cloudy surge.

With spray of scarlet fire before
The ruffled gold that round her dies,
She sails above the sleeping shore,
Across the waking skies.

The dewy beach beneath her glows;
  A pencilled beam, the light-house burns:
Full-breathed, the fragrant sea-wind blows,—
      Life to the world returns!

I stand, a spirit newly-born,
  White-limbed and pure, and strong, and fair;
The first-begotten son of Morn,
      The nursling of the air!

There, in a heap, the masks of Earth,
  The cares, the sins, the griefs, are thrown
Complete, as through diviner birth,
      I walk the sands alone.

With downy hands the winds caress,
  With frothy lips the amorous sea,
As welcoming the nakedness
      Of vanished gods, in me.

Along the ridged and sloping sand,
  Where headlands clasp the crescent cove,
A shining spirit of the land,
      A snowy shape, I move:

Or, plunged in hollow-rolling brine,
  In emerald cradles rocked and swung,
The sceptre of the sea is mine,
      And mine his endless song.

For Earth with primal dew is wet,
  Her long-lost child to rebaptize;
Her fresh, immortal Edens yet
      Their Adam recognize.

Her ancient freedom is his fee;
  Her ancient beauty is his dower:
She bares her ample breasts, that he
      May suck the milk of power.

Press on, ye hounds of life, that lurk
  So close, to seize your harried prey;
Ye fiends of Custom, Gold, and Work —
      I hear your distant bay!

And, like the Arab, when he bears
  To the insulted camel's path
His garment, which the camel tears,
      And straight forgets his wrath;

So, yonder badges of your sway,
  Life's paltry husks, to you I give:
Fall on, and in your blindness say:
      We hold the fugitive!

But leave to me this brief escape
  To simple manhood, pure and free,—
A child of God, in God's own shape,
      Between the land and sea!

THE FOUNTAIN OF TREVI.

The Coliseum lifts at night
  Its broken cells more proudly far
Than in the noonday's naked light,
  For every rent enshrines a star:
  On Cæsar's hill the royal Lar
Presides within his mansion old:
  Decay and Death no longer mar
The moon's atoning mist of gold.

Still lingering near the shrines renewed,
  We sadly, fondly, look our last;
Each trace concealed of spoilage rude
  From old or late iconoclast,
  Till, Trajan's whispering forum passed,
We hear the waters, showering bright,
  Of Trevi's ancient fountain, cast
Their woven music on the night.

The Genius of the Tiber nods
  Benign, above his tilted urn:
Kneel down and drink! the beckoning gods
  This last libation will not spurn.
  Drink, and the old enchantment learn
That hovers yet o'er Trevi's foam, —
  The promise of a sure return,
Fresh footsteps in the dust of Rome!

Kneel down and drink! the golden days
  Here lived and dreamed, shall dawn again:
Albano's hill, through purple haze,
  Again shall crown the Latin plain.
  Whatever stains of Time remain,
Left by the years that intervene,
  Lo! Trevi's fount shall toss its rain
To wash the pilgrim's forehead clean.

Drink, and depart! for Life is just:
  She gives to Faith a master-key
To ope the gate of dreams august,
  And take from joys in memory
  The certainty of joys to be:
And Trevi's basins shall be bare
  Ere we again shall fail to see
Their silver in the Roman air.

MY MISSION.

Every spirit has its mission, say the transcendental crew:
"This is mine," they cry; "Eureka! this the purpose I pursue;
For, behold, a god hath called me, and his service I shall do!

"Brother, seek thy calling likewise, thou wert destined for the same;
Sloth is sin, and toil is worship, and the soul demands an aim:
Who neglects the ordination, he shall not escape the blame."

O my ears are dinned and wearied with the clatter of the school:
Life to them is geometric, and they act by line and rule —
If there be no other wisdom, better far to be a fool!

Better far the honest nature, in its narrow path content,
Taking, with a child's acceptance, whatsoever may be sent,
Than the introverted vision, seeing Self pre-eminent.

For the spirit's proper freedom by itself may be destroyed,
Wasting, like the young Narcissus, o'er its image in the void:
Even virtue is not virtue, when too consciously enjoyed.

I am sick of canting prophets, self-elected kings that reign
Over herds of silly subjects, of their new allegiance vain:
Preaching labor, preaching duty, preaching love with lips profane.

With the holiest things they tamper, and the noblest they degrade, —
Making Life an institution, making Destiny a trade;
But the honest vice is better than the saintship they parade.

Native goodness is unconscious, asks not to be recognized;
But its baser affectation is a thing to be despised.
Only when the man is loyal to himself shall he be prized.

Take the current of your nature, make it stagnant if you will:
Dam it up to drudge forever, at the service of your mill:
Mine the rapture and the freedom of the torrent on the hill!

Straighten out your wavy borders: make a tow-path at the side:
Be the dull canal your channel, where the heavy barges glide, —
Lo, the muddy bed is tranquil, not a rapid breaks the tide!

I shall wander o'er the meadows where the fairest blossoms call:
Though the ledges seize and fling me headlong from the rocky wall,
I shall leave a rainbow hanging o'er the ruins of my fall!

I shall lead a glad existence, as I broaden down the vales,
Brimming past the regal cities, whitened with the seaward sails —
Feel the mighty pulse of ocean ere I mingle with its gales!

Vex me not with weary questions: seek no moral to deduce:
With the Present I am busy, with the Future hold a truce:
If I live the life He gave me, God will turn it to His use.

PROPOSAL.

THE violet loves a sunny bank,
  The cowslip loves the lea;
The scarlet creeper loves the elm,
      But I love — thee.

The sunshine kisses mount and vale,
  The stars, they kiss the sea;
The west winds kiss the clover bloom,
      But I kiss — thee!

The oriole weds his mottled mate;
  The lily 's bride o' the bee;
Heaven's marriage-ring is round the earth —
      Shall I wed thee?

RENUNCIATION.

I.

Words are but headstones o'er the grave of thought.
  When some gigantic passion grasps the heart
Until its powers, to utmost tension brought,
  Tug at the roots of life, no speech may start
The spell of silence. Deepest moods are dumb,
  Nor song, nor picture, nor the spells of sound
  Fathom their dark profound,
The secret of their language overcome.
But farthest, subtlest, most elusive still
  Are those dim shapes that haunt the Poet's brain,
Beyond all wish, or any grasp of will,
  That come unsought — and, sought, retreat again:
The independent fantasies that fall
  As meteors fall in clear November nights,
  Sometimes a showery burst of wayward lights,
Or singly trailing gold celestial,
Or in auroral blushes fused afar,
Drowning the steady torch of every star!

II.

There was a time when, like a child, I dreamed
  The gold lay hidden where the meteor fell:
When some divine interpretation seemed
  Unto the speech of Poets possible:
When Nature's face a mask of brightness wore,
  Beyond the brightness of the moon or sun:
The hills I knew, their skyey temples bore;
  I heard the streams to other music run.
I saw a fairer morn within the morn,
  And would have painted it for other eyes;
  I heard the harmonies of twilight skies,
The rippling idylls of the harvest corn.
The gray old mountains many a rainbow spanned,
And trumpets clamored on the ocean-sand:
The summer valleys sang a minor strain,
  Dying away in far, aerial blue,
  Until, divinely saddened through and through,
I tried their song to echo, but in vain!
Why speak of that for which there is no speech?
  Why sing of light to those who cannot see?
All that the Poet's noblest song may reach
  Is the regret for what unsung must be.

III.

I gave to Nature more than she gave back:
  The dreams that, vanished once, return no more;
  Passion that left her colder than before,
And the warm soul her stubborn features lack.
It was an echo of my heart I heard
  Sing in the sky, and chant along the sea:
My life the affluence of her own conferred,
  And gave her seeming sympathy with me.
O stars! whose light was dimmed with tears of mine!
  O sun, that smiled with more than May-day joy!
Ye do not sit upon your thrones divine
  To feed the tender fancies of a boy.
Ye see the stern eyes weep, the strong heart break,
  The courage conquered by a fate unkind,
  In your own brightness blind,
Unmoved, unchanged for any creature's sake.
The voices which encouraged me, are dumb;
  The Soul I recognized in Earth is fled;
I wait for answers which have ceased to come:
  I press the pulse of Nature: she is dead.
The early reverence I gave her fails,
  To know her apathy for human ills;
  I only see the bleak, unpitying hills,
The drear, indifferent vales,

The dark, dumb woods, the harsh, insulting sea,
The stolid sky in cold serenity, —
Cold as the ceilings are of palace-halls,
  Above their painted walls,
To some hot life, that beats in passion there,
  Barred in alone, with eyes all wet and blind,
  Which in the splendid frescoes only find
The staring mockery of their own despair!

IV.

Earth is our palace, and her zoned array
  Of forms and colors its adornments are:
She gives the soul its garments of display;
  She draws the wheels of its triumphal car.
But does the victor kiss the threshold-stone,
  Or clasp the heartless pillar at his door?
And does the bush whereon his bays have grown,
  Shine with a glossier emerald than before?
No — no! His sun is risen in kindred eyes;
  His morn, the brighter flush of friendly cheeks:
  The music of his day of triumph speaks
In human voices, and the sullen skies,
When, palm to palm, beloved pulses kiss,
Beam with the splendid sunshine of his bliss!

He gives to Earth the joy that flows from him:
  The vanquished gives her his defeat and shame:
  Her chimes, to different fates, at once proclaim
The bridal pæan and the burial hymn!

V.

O, not to know, the sunny mist that gilds
  The mountain tops, my breath had thither blown!
O, not to feel that loftiest Beauty builds
  In Man her temple, and in Man alone!
Henceforward I renounce the vain pursuit
  To find without the secret hid within, —
  To chase a phantom thin,
Masked in our own divinest attribute,
While rosy life, the beating Heart of God,
  The dayspring of the glory of the earth,
  Supplies the Poet's dearth,
If o'er its fountains move his wizard rod.
The spirit of the mountains, sought in vain,
  Sits on the forehead of the mountaineer;
The forest's voice is heard in every strain
Of hunters' bugles, and the restless main
  Sings in the sailor-songs it loves to hear.

The slender girl, beside the tropic palm,
  Stands, the completed beauty of the wild;
The sweet-brier blooms not with so sweet a balm
  Beside the cottage, as the cotter's child.
The whirls of windy fire, on desert sands,
  But faintly Man's infuriate wrath express;
The desolation of the Arctic lands
  Is warm beside his icy selfishness.
Love, passion, rapture, terror, grief, repose,
Through him alone the face of Nature knows:
There is no aspect of the changing zones
  But springs from something deeper in the heart:
  Then, let me touch its chords with tender art,
And cease to chant in wind-harp monotones!

THE QUAKER WIDOW.

I.

Thee finds me in the garden, Hannah, — come in! 'T is
kind of thee
To wait until the Friends were gone, who came to com-
fort me.
The still and quiet company a peace may give, indeed,
But blessed is the single heart that comes to us at need.

II.

Come, sit thee down! Here is the bench where Benja-
min would sit
On First-day afternoons in spring, and watch the swal-
lows flit:
He loved to smell the sprouting box, and hear the pleas-
ant bees
Go humming round the lilacs and through the apple-trees.

III.

I think he loved the spring: not that he cared for flowers: most men
Think such things foolishness, — but we were first acquainted then,
One spring: the next he spoke his mind; the third I was his wife,
And in the spring (it happened so) our children entered life.

IV.

He was but seventy-five: I did not think to lay him yet
In Kennett graveyard, where at Monthly Meeting first we met.
The Father's mercy shows in this: 't is better I should be
Picked out to bear the heavy cross — alone in age — than he.

V.

We 've lived together fifty years: it seems but one long day,
One quiet Sabbath of the heart, till he was called away;
And as we bring from Meeting-time a sweet contentment home,
So, Hannah, I have store of peace for all the days to come.

VI.

I mind (for I can tell thee now) how hard it was to
know
If I had heard the spirit right, that told me I should go;
For father had a deep concern upon his mind that day,
But mother spoke for Benjamin, — she knew what best
to say.

VII.

Then she was still: they sat a while: at last she spoke
again,
"The Lord incline thee to the right!" and "Thou shalt
have him, Jane!"
My father said. I cried. Indeed, 't was not the least
of shocks,
For Benjamin was Hicksite, and father Orthodox.

VIII.

I thought of this ten years ago, when daughter Ruth we
lost:
Her husband 's of the world, and yet I could not see her
crossed.
She wears, thee knows, the gayest gowns, she hears a
hireling priest —
Ah, dear! the cross was ours: her life 's a happy one, at
least.

IX.

Perhaps she 'll wear a plainer dress when she's as old as I, —
Would thee believe it, Hannah? once *I* felt temptation nigh!
My wedding-gown was ashen silk, too simple for my taste:
I wanted lace around the neck, and a ribbon at the waist.

X.

How strange it seemed to sit with him upon the women's side!
I did not dare to lift my eyes: I felt more fear than pride,
Till, "in the presence of the Lord," he said, and then there came
A holy strength upon my heart, and I could say the same.

XI.

I used to blush when he came near, but then I showed no sign;
With all the meeting looking on, I held his hand in mine.
It seemed my bashfulness was gone, now I was his for life:
Thee knows the feeling, Hannah, — thee, too, hast been a wife.

XII.

As home we rode, I saw no fields look half so green as ours;
The woods were coming into leaf, the meadows full of flowers;
The neighbors met us in the lane, and every face was kind, —
'T is strange how lively everything comes back upon my mind.

XIII.

I see, as plain as thee sits there, the wedding-dinner spread:
At our own table we were guests, with father at the head,
And Dinah Passmore helped us both, — 't was she stood up with me,
And Abner Jones with Benjamin, — and now they 're gone, all three!

XIV.

It is not right to wish for death; the Lord disposes best.
His Spirit comes to quiet hearts, and fits them for His rest;
And that He halved our little flock was merciful, I see:
For Benjamin has two in heaven, and two are left with me.

XV.

Eusebius never cared to farm,—'t was not his call, in truth,
And I must rent the dear old place, and go to daughter Ruth.
Thee 'll say her ways are not like mine,—young people now-a-days
Have fallen sadly off, I think, from all the good old ways.

XVI.

But Ruth is still a Friend at heart; she keeps the simple tongue,
The cheerful, kindly nature we loved when she was young;
And it was brought upon my mind, remembering her, of late,
That we on dress and outward things perhaps lay too much weight.

XVII.

I once heard Jesse Kersey say, a spirit clothed with grace,
And pure, almost, as angels are, may have a homely face.
And dress may be of less account: the Lord will look within:
The soul it is that testifies of righteousness or sin.

XVIII.

Thee must n't be too hard on Ruth: she 's anxious I
should go,
And she will do her duty as a daughter should, I know.
'T is hard to change so late in life, but we must be resigned:
The Lord looks down contentedly upon a willing mind.

ANASTASIA.

Too pure thy lips for passion's kiss;
  Too fair thy cheek love's rose to be:
The brightest dream of Beauty's bliss
  Is dark beside the dream of thee.
Thine eyes were lit from other skies;
  Thy limbs are made of purer clay;
And wandering airs of Paradise
  Before thee breathe the mists away.

Go, Angel! on thy path serene,
  The lily-garland in thy hair:
I shall not crown thee as my queen,
  Or vex thee with my hopeless prayer.
Love follows those whose dancing feet
  Like rose-leaves warm the summer sod:
Thy brow foretells the winding-sheet;
  The coffin waits thee, and the clod.

THE PALM AND THE PINE.

When Peter led the First Crusade,
A Norseman wooed an Arab maid.

He loved her lithe and palmy grace,
And the dark beauty of her face:

She loved his cheeks, so ruddy fair,
His sunny eyes and yellow hair.

He called: she left her father's tent;
She followed whereso'er he went.

She left the palms of Palestine
To sit beneath the Norland pine.

She sang the musky Orient strains
Where Winter swept the snowy plains.

Their natures met like Night and Morn
What time the morning-star is born.

The child that from their meeting grew
Hung, like that star, between the two.

The glossy night his mother shed
From her long hair was on his head:

But in its shade they saw arise
The morning of his father's eyes.

Beneath the Orient's tawny stain
Wandered the Norseman's crimson vein:

Beneath the Northern force was seen
The Arab sense, alert and keen.

His were the Viking's sinewy hands,
The arching foot of Eastern lands.

And in his soul conflicting strove
Northern indifference, Southern love;

The chastity of temperate blood,
Impetuous passion's fiery flood;

The settled faith that nothing shakes,
The jealousy a breath awakes;

The planning Reason's sober gaze,
And Fancy's meteoric blaze.

And stronger, as he grew to man,
The contradicting natures ran, —

As mingled streams from Etna flow,
One born of fire, and one of snow.

And one impelled, and one withheld,
And one obeyed, and one rebelled.

One gave him force, the other fire;
This self-control, and that desire.

One filled his heart with fierce unrest;
With peace serene the other blessed.

He knew the depth and knew the height,
The bounds of darkness and of light;

And who these far extremes has seen
Must needs know all that lies between.

So, with untaught, instinctive art,
He read the myriad-natured heart.

He met the men of many a land;
They gave their souls into his hand;

And none of them was long unknown:
The hardest lesson was his own.

But how he lived, and where, and when,
It matters not to other men;

For, as a fountain disappears,
To gush again in later years,

So hidden blood may find the day,
When centuries have rolled away;

And fresher lives betray at last
The lineage of a far-off Past.

That nature, mixed of sun and snow,
Repeats its ancient ebb and flow:

The children of the Palm and Pine
Renew their blended lives — in mine.

OVER-POSSESSION.

WITH beating heart and crowded brain,
I wait the touch of song in vain.
The coy, capricious Muse retires
Before the flame herself inspires,
And for a calmer, colder hour,
Reserves her passion and her power.

The sweetness of the autumn skies,
The light that on the landscape lies,
Where yonder sloping wood-side nods
The sunshine of the golden-rods,
The noise of children at their play,
The crickets chirping out the day,
The music breathing from the Past,
The Future's pictures, vague and vast;
The beauty men but rarely seek,
The secret truths they never speak;

The double life, — the outward show,
The hell and heaven that hide below;
The hopeless whirl of woe and wrong;
Eternal Wisdom's under-song, —
All these, by turns, possess my mind,
Yet none of these mine art can bind:
For she, my goddess, will be wooed
Alone in calm and solitude.

So, cheerfully, the weight I bear
Of hot emotions which outwear
The crowded brain, and dim the eye
Of single-sighted Poesy.
She, when the throngs around her hum,
Stands in the centre, blind and dumb;
But to the One unveils her charms,
And clasps him in immortal arms.

ON LEAVING CALIFORNIA.

O FAIR young land, the youngest, fairest far
Of which our world can boast, —
Whose guardian planet, Evening's silver star,
Illumes thy golden coast, —

How art thou conquered, tamed in all the pride
Of savage beauty still!
How brought, O panther of the splendid hide,
To know thy master's will!

No more thou sittest on thy tawny hills
In indolent repose;
Or pour'st the crystal of a thousand rills
Down from thy house of snows.

But where the wild-oats wrapped thy knees in gold,
    The ploughman drives his share,
And where, through cañons deep, thy streams are rolled,
    The miner's arm is bare.

Yet in thy lap, thus rudely rent and torn,
    A nobler seed shall be:
Mother of mighty men, thou shalt not mourn
    Thy lost virginity!

Thy human children shall restore the grace
    Gone with thy fallen pines:
The wild, barbaric beauty of thy face
    Shall round to classic lines.

And Order, Justice, Social Law shall curb
    Thy untamed energies;
And Art, and Science, with their dreams superb,
    Replace thine ancient ease.

The marble, sleeping in thy mountains now,
    Shall live in sculptures rare;
Thy native oak shall crown the sage's brow,—
    Thy bay, the poet's hair.

Thy tawny hills shall bleed their purple wine,
    Thy valleys yield their oil ;
And Music, with her eloquence divine,
    Persuade thy sons to toil.

Till Hesper, as he trims his silver beam,
    No happier land shall see,
And Earth shall find her old Arcadian dream
    Restored again in thee!

EUPHORION.

"I will not longer
Earth-bound linger:
Loosen your hold on
Hand and on ringlet,
Girdle and garment;
Leave them: they 're mine!"

"Bethink thee, bethink thee
To whom thou belongest!
Say, wouldst thou wound us,
Rudely destroying
Threefold the beauty, —
Mine, his, and thine?"

FAUST, — SECOND PART.

NAY, fold your arms, beloved Friends,
Above the hearts that vainly beat!
Or catch the rainbow where it bends,
And find your darling at its feet;

Or fix the fountain's varying shape,
The sunset-cloud's elusive dye,
The speech of winds that round the cape
Make music to the sea and sky:

So may you summon from the air
  The loveliness that vanished hence,
And Twilight give his beauteous hair,
  And Morning give his countenance,

And Life about his being clasp
  Her rosy girdle once again: —
But no! let go your stubborn grasp
  On some wild hope, and take your pain!

For, through the crystal of your tears,
  His love and beauty fairer shine;
The shadows of advancing years
  Draw back, and leave him all divine.

And Death, that took him, cannot claim
  The smallest vesture of his birth, —
The little life, a dancing flame
  That hovered o'er the hills of earth, —

The finer soul, that unto ours
  A subtle perfume seemed to be,
Like incense blown from April flowers
  Beside the scarred and stormy tree, —

The wondering eyes, that ever saw
  Some fleeting mystery in the air,
And felt the stars of evening draw
  His heart to silence, childhood's prayer!

Our suns were all too fierce for him;
  Our rude winds pierced him through and through:
But Heaven has valleys cool and dim,
  And boscage sweet with starry dew.

There knowledge breathes in balmy air,
  Not wrung, as here, with panting breast:
The wisdom born of toil you share;
  But he, the wisdom born of rest.

For every picture here that slept,
  A living canvas is unrolled;
The silent harp he might have swept
  Leans to his touch its strings of gold.

Believe, dear Friends, they murmur still
  Some sweet accord to those you play,
That happier winds of Eden thrill
  With echoes of the earthly lay;

That he, for every triumph won,
  Whereto your poet-souls aspire,
Sees opening, in that perfect sun,
  Another blossom's bud of fire!

Each song, of Love and Sorrow born,
  Another flower to crown your boy, —
Each shadow here his ray of morn,
  Till Grief shall clasp the hand of Joy!

SOLDIER'S SONG.

FROM "FAUST."

CASTLES with lofty
  Ramparts and towers, —
Maidens disdainful
  In Beauty's array, —
  All shall be ours!
Bold is the venture,
  Splendid the pay!

Lads, let the trumpets
  For us be sueing,
Calling to pleasure,
  Calling to ruin!

Stormy our life is ;
  Such is its boon :
Maidens and castles
  Capitulate soon.
Bold is the venture,
  Splendid the pay !
And the soldiers go marching,
  Marching away.

THE SHEPHERD'S LAMENT.

FROM GOETHE.

Up yonder on the mountain
   A thousand times I stand,
Leant on my crook, and gazing
   Down on the valley-land.

I follow the flock to the pasture;
   My little dog watches them still:
I have come below, but I know not
   How I descended the hill.

The beautiful meadow is covered
   With blossoms of every hue;
I pluck them, alas! without knowing
   Whom I shall give them to.

I seek, in the rain and the tempest,
  A refuge under the tree:
Yonder the doors are fastened,
  And all is a dream to me.

Right over the roof of the dwelling
  I see a rainbow stand;
But she has departed forever,
  And gone far out in the land.

Far out in the land, and farther, —
  Perhaps to an alien shore:
Go forward, ye sheep! go forward, —
  The heart of the shepherd is sore.

THE GARDEN OF ROSES.

FROM UHLAND.

Of the beautiful Garden of Roses
  I will sing, with your gracious leave:
There the dames walked forth at morning,
  And the heroes fought at eve.

"My Lord is King of the country,
  But I am the Garden's Queen;
His crown with the red gold sparkles,
  And mine with the rose's sheen.

"So hear me, ye youthful gallants,
  My favorite guardsmen three;
The garden is free to the maidens,
  To the knights it must not be.

" They would trample my beautiful roses,
And bring me trouble enow," —
Said the Queen, as she walked in the morning,
With the garland on her brow.

Then went the three young gallants
And guarded the gate about;
And peacefully blossomed the roses
And sent their odors out.

Now came three fair young maidens,
Virgins that knew not sin:
" Ye guardsmen, ye gallant three guardsmen,
Open, and let us in!"

And when they had gathered the roses,
They spake, with looks forlorn:
" What makes our hands so bloody?
Is it the prick of the thorn?"

And still the three young gallants
Guarded the gate about,
And peacefully blossomed the roses,
And sent their odors out.

Now came upon prancing stallions
  Three lawless knights, and cried:
"Ye guardsmen, ye surly three guardsmen,
  Open the portal wide!"

"The portal is shut and bolted:
  Our naked swords will teach
That the price of the roses is costly;
  Ye must pay a wound for each!"

Then fought the knights and the gallants,
  But the knights had the victory,
And the roses were torn and trampled,
  And died with the guardsmen three.

And when the evening darkened,
  The Queen came by with her train:
"Now that my roses are trampled
  And my faithful guardsmen slain,

"I will lay them on leaves of roses,
  And bury them solemnly:
And where was the Garden of Roses,
  The Garden of Lilies shall be.

"But who will watch my lilies,
  When their blossoms open white?
By day the sun shall be sentry,
  And the moon and the stars by night!"

THE THREE SONGS.

FROM UHLAND.

King Siegfried sat in his lofty hall:
"Ye harpers! who sings the best song of all?"
Then a youth stepped forth with a scornful lip,
The harp in his hand, and the sword at his hip.

"Three songs I know; but this first song
Thou, O King! hast forgotten long:
Thou hast stabbed my brother with murderous hand —
Hast stabbed my brother with murderous hand!

"The second song I learned aright
In the midst of a dark and stormy night:
Thou must fight with me for life or death —
Must fight with me for life or death!"

On the banquet-table he laid his harp,
And they both drew out their swords so sharp;
And they fought in the sight of the harpers all,
Till the King sank dead in the lofty hall.

"And now for the third, the proudest, best!
I shall sing it, sing it, and never rest:
King Siegfried lies in his red, red blood —
Siegfried lies in his red, red blood!"

THE END.

Cambridge: Stereotyped and Printed by Welch, Bigelow, & Co.

www.ingramcontent.com/pod-product-compliance
Lightning Source LLC
LaVergne TN
LVHW011216110826
845150LV00006B/1443

* 9 7 8 1 4 2 5 5 1 7 0 5 2 *